As I Was Thinking . . .

Observations and Thoughts on International Business and Trade

As I Was Thinking . . .

Observations and Thoughts on International Business and Trade

Michael R. Czinkota
The McDonough School of Business,
Georgetown University,
Washington D.C., U S A

BEP BUSINESS EXPERT PRESS

First published in 2015 by
Business Expert Press, LLC
222 East 46th Street, New York, NY 10017
www.businessexpertpress.com

ISBN-13: 978-1-63157-160-2 (paperback)
ISBN-13: 978-1-63157-161-9 (e-book)

Business Expert Press International Business Collection

Collection ISSN: 1948-2752 (print)
Collection ISSN: 1948-2760 (electronic)

Cover and interior design by S4Carlisle Publishing Services
Private Ltd., Chennai, India

First edition: 2015

10 9 8 7 6 5 4 3 2 1

Printed in the United States of America.

Dedication

To Margaret my quinceañera, horse woman.

Introduction

This compilation of articles and editorials published by Professor Czinkota in news media worldwide contains thoughtful insight into core dimensions of international business and trade. The vast array of themes reflects how international business reaches every corner of our world today. This volume makes much of this complexity more accessible by presenting the topics, its analysis and controversies, and possible new directions in a few pages—just enough for bed time reading. Also, each analysis is accompanied by t cartoon, developed by Czinkota and award winning cartoonist David Clark. Through the parsimonious use of the word and the frequent offer of insightful cartoons, we hope to enhance understanding and appreciation of the international trade and investment environment.

We live in a global community in many ways; however, many sectors need to catch up to these approaches—such as international marketing and trade policies. Additionally, an international market only functions through trust and relationships between merchants and companies. In spite of better communications across great distances, business relationships are still as important as ever, and will not be disappearing any time soon.

Political and international affairs directly impact every form of business. However, readers are bombarded with a colossal volume of reports and articles, which can be overwhelming. Therefore, in spite of progress in transparency, it becomes increasingly burdensome to understand the consequences of a global market. This is why we offer these short commentaries, editorials, and cartoons to encourage comprehension of and thinking about the most important and relevant topics today.

Most people fail to recognize that they play a role in international trade. The vast majority of purchases made by consumers, from household goods to clothes to automobiles, incorporate parts that originate from different nations. This not only illustrates how integrated the global economy has become, but shows how international trade leads to greater efficiency. As nations continue to export goods that they specialize in, the input cost for nearly every good and service imaginable declines.

In addition, advances in shipping allow consumers to make international purchases through online forums and websites and have it sent directly to their home. This provides the consumer with a broader array of options, leading to a more satisfied consumer.

People enjoy the idea of free trade, but do not necessarily accept the consequences that come along as a part of it. For many, internationalization denotes the ability to purchase satisfactory goods for a very low price. However, these goods will often come from other nations, which leads to a lower demand for the local industry output. This is a tradeoff that comes with the reality of free trade but reform strikes fear in the hearts of individuals. Additionally, the role of the government has come into question in recent years, especially with regards to downturns in the economy. Some insist that government should intervene to help create jobs, while others argue that the government has already overstepped its boundaries in terms of everyday individual lives. The articles of this book touch on the natural ebb and flow in every economy and how set-backs actually bring about innovation and often inspire new business policies and practices that increase efficiency. Recent recessions do not signal a decline on the world stage, but rather an opportunity to move forward with new determination and pursue different frontiers. At the same time, if we demand that government provides the greatest protection possible, then we have to be willing to give up a certain amount of privacy, as is discussed in the section about economic growth and freedom.

This book also outlines some of the far-reaching consequences that wars, international conflict, and overall lack of trust can have on business relationships and therefore trade. From the increasing conflict in the Middle East, to the current situation between Russian and Ukraine, to global terrorism, all of these events cause people to divert investments elsewhere, which can have a large economic and financial impact.

This book outlines important aspects of international business, and often does so with a bit of humor and in an entertaining manner. Do read this book, it will be fun, easy, and worthwhile.

My thoughts go to . . .

In completing this work, I thank the members of my research team. In particular Kimberly Boeckmann, Alice Lu, Courtlyn Cook, and all my colleagues and collaborators. Gratitude is also due to my Georgetown colleagues, Professor Ronkainen, Professor Cooke, and Professor Skuba. Their insights and debates keep international business alive at Georgetown's McDonough School of Business. I am also thankful to the economic kindness of the editors and newspapers who have given me permission to reprint my articles. Heartfelt thanks to David Clark, the award-winning artist who has provided the visual stimuli for this book and my annual calendar. Most of all, I am grateful to my wife Ilona Czinkota who is a major arbiter for the quality of my writings. Early or late in the day, she is willing to provide suggestions. My daughter Margaret comments as well with much enthusiasm and interest. Both mother and daughter are great sounding boards and come up with excellent questions and solutions. Thanks to all of you!

Michael R. Czinkota
Washington, DC
January 1, 2015

Foreword

By Donald Manzullo, (Fmr) Chair, House Small Business Committee and Subcommittee on Asia

So often we see threads in our world that remain unraveled and never connected. International business and trade is a good example. Professor Michael Czinkota of McDonough School of Business at Georgetown University, Washington, D.C., has always seen the greater context of international business and trade, as exemplified in the many books he has published on the topic.

A friend of mine for many years, Professor Czinkota is a voice for simplifying a confusing and potentially terrifying subject called international trade. His goal is to help people sell products overseas by recasting the barriers to trade in terms of challenges that can in many cases be overcome with a little thought and elbow grease. At the same time, he demonstrates the absolute necessity of understanding the basic concepts of commerce, manufacturing, education, innovation, and the role of government (which should be limited in his universe).

In his latest publication, Professor Czinkota does what he does best: he weaves together theory and practice of international business and trade. This book compiles previously published short essays (many of which are co-authored with specialists in various fields). A cartoon – that's right, a cartoon! – appears at the beginning of each essay. While not common in most academic publications, the cartoons show readers that the content that follows is more than a boring yawn! In fact, Czinkota's essays showcase those attributes that are absolutely essential for a nation to lead and for a people to succeed in the rough-and-tumble world of international business.

He unfolds his work by categorizing his essays into five general areas.

In section one, "On Commerce and Trade," Professor Czinkota defines effective trade strategy as "world leadership." A nation is successful, he claims, because of its manufacturing of goods, productions of services and trade policy. His disdain for protectionism is apparent in an essay in which he opposes President George W. Bush's steel policy because of its overall impact on U.S. manufacturing. Importantly, he underscores that world leadership is not based on rhetoric, but on cutting-edge manufacturing and services and the ability to sell one's product around the world.

Czinkota, an unabashed free-market pundit, is not averse to a limited government role in increasing trade, especially programs not otherwise available in the private sector. Nevertheless, he maintains that the government's influence must be exercised correctly; thus, in one essay, he criticizes the Obama administration for trying to "streamline" exporting agencies in a manner that will not work. Czinkota is a non-partisan critic of those government officials who seem not to understand the political and economic impact of international trade: with steel tariffs, it was the Bush Administration; on "reorganization" it is the Obama Administration.

Czinkota also demonstrates the importance of increasing our exports as a way of adding to our gross domestic product (GDP). For some, this will seem like an obvious assertion; they may be amazed he has to state it at all. The European Union's and Chinese exports are many times greater than those of the United States, as a proportion of their GDP. The time has come the time has come for Americans to heed his admonition!

The essays in this book range widely in focus: from the search for honorable international partners, to the Chinese purchase of Smithfield Foods, to the rise of consumer power in terms of sustainability and conservation. Throughout all, the professor substantiates his claim that international trade impacts everybody and that trade is not just *a* tool but *the* tool of national wealth and leadership.

In the section on "Innovation in Today's Global Community" Czinkota offers a wide-ranging analysis of numerous concepts, including a discussion of the synergies among manufacturing, marketing, and finance. Businesses that produce good products, he claims, need to be able to meet the challenges of selling their product and financing their operations without locking themselves into one-size-fits-all solutions. Today, real-time information has upended yesterday's mindset of simply relying on quality and reputation for sales. The author warns that, due to technology's rise, consumers often assume the quality of product, but need to be informed as to *why* Product A is preferable to Product B.

Another essay in this section—co-authored by Czinkota's brother, Thomas—challenges the process of education today. Education, the authors claim, is not only *what* is taught but *how* it is taught. Challenge the child to understand *why* he should learn, and in turn, he will. Just don't shove it down his throat and say, "You'll need this for college."

In section three, on "Daily Life and International Affairs," Czinkota explores product branding, a topic similar to, yet distinct from, marketing, which he discussed in the preceding section. Branding defines *who* you are; marketing determines *how* you are perceived. Like marketing, branding is a tool for the present or prospective international seller, and Czinkota explains this tool in terms of how others have utilized it. In one essay, Czinkota compares brand satisfaction with a romantic relationship. Using the example of the 2012 Royal Wedding of Prince William and Kate Middleton—which millions around the world watched on TV—he points out that "love does conquer all"; the same, he says, is true of a product's sales. Admitting that the consumer does not explicitly expect a love affair with the product he or she buys, Czinkota nevertheless points out the truth of the old fairy tale line "they lived happily ever after": a happy marriage (of sorts) results when a consumer buys and loves the product.

Section four focuses on "Business and Conflict." Czinkota examines the impact of global terrorism on international business practices and considers respectable and responsive corporate reaction thereto. The author rightly observes that the object of the terrorists is to disrupt America and others by committing grand acts of violence. He challenges companies with this provocative statement: "Perhaps the best hope for a brighter future in troubled regions is business that, in addition to expanding profits, meets the social and economic needs of local stakeholders." This is capitalist theory at its best: Czinkota demonstrates that the pursuit of profit need not result in exploitation, and affirms that "doing the right thing" usually leads to success. It is refreshing to hear an expert on trade reflect on morality in business; we need more voices like that in the marketplace.

The fifth and final section centers on "Freedom and Economic Growth." Czinkota reminds us of the cultural differences among nations and at times sounds more like a professor of sociology than business. Ultimately, this approach serves to remind readers that, in the end, business is all about people. It suggests that perhaps we should look at world commerce through the eyes of people in general as opposed to politicians, professors, and businesspeople.

In addition to its scholarly insight and wisdom, Czinkota's book is fun to read, and loaded with anecdotes that reduce the theoretical to the practical so that every player—the manufacturer, exporter, and consumer—can glean real-life application.

He's a first class professor who gets it.

Washington DC. November 19, 2014

Content

SECTION 1

On Commerce and Trade

The Cost of Free Trade

Originally Published by Marketing Management: July–August 2003

U.S. President George W. Bush's decision to impose tariffs on steel imports into the United States has been decried as a politically motivated and economically ruinous move that marks the end of free trade and initiates a battle in the World Trade Organization.

We could, of course, dispatch our experts again to WTO hearings and start the traditional international charges and countercharges. The better alternative is to use this occasion to informally delineate a U.S. trade strategy that lets our industry and foreign friends know where we stand and where we are headed. Doing so will provide predictability to the market and consistency to our decision-making, both of which will increase market confidence.

Here are the components of our trade strategy: First is world leadership. The U.S. carries the leadership mantle due to astute policymaking, a willingness to contribute to the greater global good, and fortuitous developments in history. Some of our allies desire to be the leaders when it comes to international economic standards but are happy to let us bear the burden of armed conflict or the risk of terrorism. Global leadership is not a partitionable function, applicable to only a few issues: It is all encompassing.

Next are the benefits of leadership. We don't know how long the currently unassailable position of the U.S. will last, but world history tells us that positions can change. Past leadership is good for prominence in the history books, or for minor privileges, such as Greece's position of first flag carrier during the Olympics. Past accomplishments do little when it comes to resources or influence. Just think, in 1948 the U.S. almost launched the International Trade Organization, which would have streamlined global commerce. We didn't push hard then and the effort failed. It took almost 50 years to relaunch such an institution—now called the World Trade Organization, which still does not have the same strengths as the ITO would have had. It is important to make hay while the sun shines. Britain, long in decline, was able to draw on the resources acquired during the height of empire for more than half a century. The U.S. will get things done now and also acquire bankable resources for a rainy day.

Third, we need ongoing international help in counting our blessings when it comes to free trade. Every elected official has many vocal constituents recount vivid tales of travails caused by imports. The positive effects caused by free trade are not self-evident; they must be explained, defined and provided by industry and our trading partners on a regular basis, particularly when it comes to jobs. As far as congressional votes go, trade-related employment effects are the currency of the realm.

Fourth, in a global world, local issues are important. When it comes to trade, expectations of a perfect track record may be the enemy of good achievements. Trade is only one component of the mosaic of mankind's activity. Policy needs to reflect the broad scope of human desires and needs. The steel decision needs to be seen in such a context. There is a political price tag associated with strong U.S. support of free trade. The rare and limited protection of a domestic industry with much leverage is such a price.

During the anthrax scare, the U.S. government negotiated rather harshly with Bayer, the producer of Cipro. Some claimed that such an approach was in violation of long-standing support for intellectual property rights. Realistically, it is an emergency-appropriate deviation from the established routine, a necessary price of past and future enforcement consistency.

Fifth, our trade strategy is balanced. The fact that jobs matter also helps the free traders. As the chairman of the congressional House Small Business Committee stated: "I will watch very carefully how the steel tariffs affect the steel users and exporters in my district. And if jobs get lost, I will pounce!" Our representatives have become familiar with global concerns. In the future, international trade actions will perhaps mainly be addressed domestically, after a battle between, say, sugar vs. steel interests.

Was the steel decision political? Of course it was, in the sense of exercising the art of compromise. The decision also defines new boundaries. It has a clear context, provides direction and promises containment. It demonstrates U.S. leadership and, simultaneously, strengthens the world trade framework.

Trade Policy and International Marketing

(With Charles Skuba)

Originally Published by Marketing Management

THE UNITED STATES IS IN a vulnerable position when it comes to international trade. Since 1975, it has been importing more goods than it has been exporting, therefore running a continuous merchandise trade deficit. Even though overall U.S. exports surpassed $1 trillion in 2001, the deficit in the trade of goods was more than $426 billion. Ongoing annual trade deficits of this magnitude are unsustainable in the long run. Such deficits add to the U.S. international debt, which must be serviced through interest payments and eventually perhaps even repaid. Therefore, an export performance by U.S. firms that matches or even exceeds our imports will become crucial.

Furthermore, exports are also an important contributor to national employment. We estimate that $1 billion of exports supports the creation, on average, of about 11,500 jobs. In its latest benchmark study, the U.S. Department of Commerce reports there were more than 8 million U.S. jobs sustained by the export of manufactured goods, which ties one out of every five U.S. manufacturing jobs directly or indirectly to exports. For example, in the state of Illinois alone, more than 360,000 jobs were linked to manufactured exports. An increase in exports can therefore be a key factor in maintaining domestic job growth.

Many see the global market as the exclusive realm of large, multinational corporations. Overlooked are the hundreds of thousands of smaller firms that have been fueling a U.S. export boom, which has supported the economy in times of limited domestic growth. The latest information from the trade data project at the Department of Commerce indicates that, between 1987 and 1999, the number of U.S. firms that export at least occasionally has more than tripled to more than 231,000. Almost 97% of these exporters were small or mid-sized companies.

The reason for the export success of smaller firms lies in the new determinants of competitiveness, as framed by the wishes and needs of the foreign buyers. Other than price, buyers today also expect an excellent product fit, high levels of corporate responsiveness, a substantial service orientation, and high corporate commitment. Small and mid-sized firms stack up well on all these dimensions, compared to their larger brethren, and may even have a competitive advantage.

Corporate Vulnerabilities

In spite of many advantages, smaller firms face major obstacles to international market prosperity.

Financial issues. All firms worry about getting paid when they ship their merchandise abroad, but small and mid-sized exporters are particularly at risk. They need financing to cover the time lag between shipping and payment receipts as well as to offer credit to buyers. Longer distances, slower transportation, and more accommodating payment terms abroad make international transactions more expensive. These transactions also require more capital and represent a larger portion of the firm's resources than do domestic transactions. In addition, due to their size, international shipments often represent a larger degree of risk than smaller firms are willing or able to tolerate.

Exchange rate changes present a major source of vulnerability. Time passes between the initiation of an international transaction and its consummation. During that time, the firm is exposed to the effects of currency shifts. Major changes of currency value can transform a good business transaction into a money-losing one.

One particular issue U.S. exporters must cope with is the competition from the Euro zone and its currency volatility. The Euro is the new international trade currency the European Union implemented widely on in 2002. Even though originally introduced at a value slightly higher than the dollar, the Euro was valued at only .88 during most of 2002. Consequently, U.S. imports from Europe became cheaper, but U.S. exporters found it more difficult to compete. During the latter part of last year, the Euro rose in value and now exceeds the dollar. However, this has mainly been a function of different interest rate policies, which have been guided by a flexible U.S. Fed and a very unyielding European Central Bank. Changes in bank leadership, which appear quite likely, may presage new policies and a return to a rapidly rising dollar.

Smaller firms also lack the unfettered access to global capital markets that large firms have. They still rely very heavily on mainly domestic or even local sources of money. As a result, they don't benefit from the low-cost opportunities of global capital and are not diversified enough in their sources of funds to cope with local interest rate inefficiencies. Given the increasing commoditization of goods, price shifts resulting from interest or exchange rate changes may critically affect the firm's competitiveness and profits.

Supply chain management. Key concerns here are the development of contacts, relationships, and networks with suppliers and the forging of a systems linkage with intermediaries and customers. In addition, there are the logistics of arranging transportation, determining transport rates, handling documentation, obtaining financial information, coordinating distribution, packaging, and obtaining insurance. The logistics are often handled by intermediaries, such as freight forwarders. This area also includes the overseas servicing of exports, where the firm needs to accommodate returns and provide parts, repair service, and technical advice. Often the solution is to open a servicing or distribution office abroad. Timely communication among the different members of the supply chain is crucial if a firm is to perform competitively. Here again, small and mid-sized firms are particularly vulnerable since they may need to invest heavily in information technology--a major capital outlay. They don't have the clout of large firms that can require their international supply chain members to adapt to a standardized information system. Smaller firms have to adapt to multiple systems and find ways to make them internationally compatible--incurring additional expenses and technical difficulties.

Firms that developed elaborate just-in-time delivery systems for their international shipments were also severely affected by the border and port closures during the days following the terrorist attacks on the United States. Together with their service providers, they continue to be affected by the increased security measures. Firms now need to focus on internal security and must demonstrate to third parties how much more security-oriented they've become. In many instances, government authorities require evidence of threat-reduction efforts to speed things along. Insurance companies have increased their premiums substantially in response to new definitions of risk. Unless policy holders take major steps to reduce such risk (or assume some of it themselves), they are likely to suffer from continued premium increases.

Regulatory issues. Another key vulnerability consists of legal procedures and typically covers government red tape, product liability, licensing, and customs/duty issues. Here, small and mid-sized firms are particularly exposed to changing government policies. The September 11 terrorist attacks have profoundly affected the administration of U.S. export controls and customs procedures. While larger firms have the benefit of a fully staffed department that deals with regulatory affairs, smaller exporters often face new and unfamiliar territory. For them, export control regulations are more burdensome. In addition, customs classifications and rules may require the hiring of specialists who ensure that shipments go out and come in properly reported and on time.

On the regulatory side, U.S. firms also are exposed to the vicissitudes of trade policy. Market access and market performance issues should be taken up in the Doha Round, the new conference of trade liberalization negotiations due to conclude by 2005. However, in existing trade disputes, our firms are also threatened by the retaliatory measures taken by trade adversaries overseas. Even though a conflict may be totally unrelated to their industry, U.S. manufacturers are vulnerable to foreign trade policy actions specifically designed to elicit the largest amount of pain from their victims. For example, when European countries or China react to U.S. import duties on foreign steel products, they do so by placing new (or higher) tariffs on a wide range of U.S. products. This makes many U.S. firms, including smaller producers, noncompetitive in these markets. They, in effect, pay the price for the U.S. protection of the domestic steel industry.

Market contact. Small to mid-sized firms need to cope with advertising, sales effort, and obtaining marketing information. They also need to develop foreign market intelligence on the location of markets, trade restrictions, and competitive conditions overseas. For large firms, such activities are often part of market expansion, where additional activities are carried out in already familiar territory. Small and mid-sized firms, however, are often still at the level of international market entry, where each step requires the dedication of new resources to unfamiliar tasks. It bears remembering that any new entrant into the international market must not only match, but must exceed by far, the capabilities of the local competition overseas. After all, apart from needing to find the spare capacity among its management resources, which permits a corporate focus on and commitment to exports, the newcomer must also carry all the transaction costs associated with the internationalization process. These start with the cost of shipping and special packaging and include duties and other special international burdens.

All these obstacles, both real and perceived, can prevent firms from exporting. Many managers often see only the risks involved rather than the opportunities the international market can present. As a result, the United States still under-exports when compared to other nations. U.S. merchandise exports comprise only 11% of GDP, compared to 28.3% for Germany and 25.4% for the United Kingdom. On a per capita basis, in 2000 the United Kingdom exported $6,226 for every man, woman, and child. The figure for Germany was $7,498, and for the United States, only $3,878.

Opportunities for Support

Currently, U.S. export performance is insufficient given its potential. Many small and medium-sized exporters are too complacent to globalize because they're either content with a vast domestic market or fear the complexity of selling abroad. Firms that do consider global opportunities appear to be unwilling to initiate major expansions of their operations abroad because of their real and perceived risk in the international market.

One core business concern is financing. On the positive side, private lenders of trade finance are becoming more active in the United States, but they often lend at relatively high rates. U.S. exporters have the benefit of many effective federal and state government programs, such as the working capital guarantee program by the Export Import Bank of the United States (Eximbank), which provides financing assistance. There are several programs specifically designed to help small business exporters. Still there needs to be a continuous emphasis on small business lending support and a responsible adaptation of credit criteria for the conditions of small and medium-sized enterprises. For example, small and mid-sized firms often can't afford to provide all the detailed evaluations and documentations lenders ideally want to see.

Of key relevance is a stable financial environment, both domestically and internationally. Small and mid-sized firms can cope with changing conditions. However, the speed of change can severely influence or even destroy the profitability of operations. Any policy measures that affect the access to and the cost of capital of smaller firms or the exchange rate of the dollar should specifically take into account the consequences and burden that such steps would impose on U.S. exporters.

Think Internationally

In time, nearly every firm will be an international marketer, by default if not by design. As globalization expands, companies will have no place to hide. New foreign competition in their own backyards will force firms to think internationally, if only defensively. Improving offerings to combat new rivals at home might well generate new demand for a firm's goods in foreign markets. As online marketplaces bring together buyers and sellers from all over the world quickly and efficiently, Internet search engines will lead prospective customers to company Web sites, even those designed for domestic buyers only.

From most perspectives, world trade conducted by savvy international marketers is the prerequisite to global growth, prosperity, and freedom for all peoples. And for companies themselves, the choice is clear: Have lunch or be lunch.

Reorganize, But Spare Agencies That Count

(With Don Bonker)

Originally Published in the Roll Call—March 8, 2012

In this year's presidential election, the dominant issues should be creating jobs and growing the economy. The Republicans are championing tax cuts, deregulation and elimination of government agencies. President Barack Obama and the Democrats prefer more federal spending.

Rhetoric may win votes, but the fact is that neither side is addressing the key issue. How we compete in today's global economy will do more to get America out of this economic slump than arguing about tax reductions or more stimulus spending.

Obama's initiative to "streamline" government services by merging several agencies under a new department charged with overseeing trade and investment programs has merit but not in the form he recently presented it.

Three of the agencies targeted were created a half-century ago with distinct mandates.

The Export-Import Bank, established in 1952 to help Russia enter U.S. markets, has evolved as a major provider of financial assistance (mostly loan guarantees) to American companies exporting goods and services. The Overseas Private Investment Corp. and the U.S. Trade and Development Agency were set up within the State Department to leverage U.S. investments to help the economies of developing countries.

For U.S. exporters, these are the critical agencies. They provide the financial assistance, loan guarantees, risk insurance, feasibility studies and other services that are essential. Other countries are far more generous in supporting their industries in pursuit of foreign markets, often placing U.S. companies at a disadvantage.

The two other agencies to be merged are the Small Business Administration and the U.S. Trade Representative.

The SBA brings value in that it has regional offices that could more readily make available export services to U.S. companies.

The idea of merging USTR with other agencies has already drawn heavy criticism from the trade community and Capitol Hill, and for good reason. USTR's activity is international in its outlook and mission. Its mandate is to conduct trade negotiations and convince trading partners to comply with laws and preferences and to represent the U.S. at the World Trade Organization. This relatively small office should not be bureaucratized if it is to maintain its independence and credibility, domestically and internationally.

Most puzzling in the president's announcement is the fate of the Department of Commerce.

The National Oceanic and Atmospheric Administration is the behemoth in the department and should be rightly split off and housed at the Department of Interior. Yet, Commerce houses agencies that provide a variety of services to American exporters, including the U.S. Commercial Services (its offices in U.S. embassies provide valuable assistance to American companies), the International Trade Administration and the Bureau of Industry and Security.

Midsize American companies need such programs if they are to be competitive. The reality of dealing in international markets, often called "burden of foreignness," is that they must cope with foreign currencies, shipping and distribution outlets, custom regulations, language and cultural differences.

The president's reorganization plan implies that the Department of Commerce will be streamlined out of business. There is nothing bold or even unique about proposing the dismemberment of the Commerce Department. It has been done before. In 1913, its labor section became the Department of Labor. In 1966, its transportation office became the Department of Transportation. Like a modern-day hydra, whenever a head is cut off, it is replaced by new ones.

The Department of Commerce's newly appointed head will be limited in his influence at the table. A predictable turf battle of jurisdiction will be waged on Capitol Hill. The department's bureaus and activities will be up for grabs, picked over like a cadaver in the desert, without achieving the efficiency sought by the White House.

Commerce needs a makeover, but it should not cease to exist. The purpose of the reorganization should be U.S. competitiveness, not job elimination.

If it is important to change the name, call it the Department of Industry and Trade, but place all the trade-related functions under one roof.

The Commerce Department should be the beacon light on the hill that radiates entrepreneurialism, and U.S. companies seeking export assistance should not even encounter a whiff of bureaucracy that is often more frustrating than helpful.

Exports and Imports for US Manufacturers

(With Don Manzullo)

Originally Published by The Washington Times: May 27, 2003

U.S. manufacturing needs policy help, now. Low exports and a surge of imports have left the sector vulnerable, endangering future economic progress and hollowing out our defense industrial base.

Our trade deficits for goods with Mexico, Germany, Japan, and China are huge and getting bigger. Last year, the U.S. deficit with just China was $103 billion. We have an imbalance of $111 billion in motor vehicles alone. The imbalance is actually greater than even we can quantify, because there is no way to measure the amount of foreign parts in U.S. exported goods.

U.S. firms clearly don't do enough exporting. It's not that they don't want to. There are simply too many bureaucratic obstacles for many of them to overcome. Compared to almost 34 percent for the European Union and 26 percent for China, U.S. exports pale, with only 11 percent of total gross domestic product. Almost half of all import shipments come from foreign affiliates, captive suppliers and U.S. subsidiaries.

The peril is apparent: When the manufacturing sector disappears, the effects go beyond lost jobs. Replacement parts become unavailable. Product re-orders take weeks rather than days. Do we really want to depend on old friends abroad for the rapid supply of manufactures critical to national security?

Manufacturing migration affects innovation and market responsiveness. By staying close to market and using emerging technologies in new products, companies gain experience and boost performance. When production is moved offshore, the rapid-response capability to market demands is dulled. A good example is what is happening with the SARS virus and its impact on global supply chains. The April 22, 2003 issue of Investor's Business Daily states "the threat of supply chain disruptions from China, Taiwan, Singapore and Indonesia is real. . . Computer, electronics, apparel and other firms are edgy about supply-chain troubles as their Asian partners send thousands of workers home and shut assembly lines."

When manufacturing firms close up shop, file for bankruptcy protection or move operations overseas, it's Americans who lose. We lose local expertise and strong competition. The once-demanding customers for American made products now become demanding customers for foreign-made goods.

Moving manufacturing overseas will also have other long-term consequences. A study at Temple University has found that the creation of new technology is a painstaking learning process of continual adjustment as new productive methods are tested. It is the small and medium manufacturers that create 55 percent of workplace innovations. The shifts abroad may eradicate technology and design and process advantages, placing U.S. firms and the country at further, future disadvantage.

Long-term economic adjustment does little for the unemployed overwhelmed by immediate needs. We don't think the answer is more legislation against countries and industries that account for substantial imbalances. That substitutes government judgment for market direction, which is not a very successful and sustainable replacement. Typically, prices rise disproportionately, consumers are deprived of desirable goods and firms find their ability to export undermined.

Policy must encourage existing market activities. Firms seeking export assistance should be supported by one personal export officer [PEXO], regardless of which agency handles the details. At our suggestion, the administration recently created an interagency training program to improve trade facilitation services for small businesses bewildered by the process and number of government forms, agencies, and participants. The Trade Promotion Coordinating Committee, composed of the 19 federal agencies that facilitate trade, conducted the first interagency seminar for PEXOs in January 2003.

There also needs to be more support for the fusion of goods, services and global networks. Consider how the automotive industry has combined airbags, the global positioning system and car telephones. Car manufacturers offer a new level of passenger assistance that can independently notify emergency services in case of an accident. Such fusions of readily available products are crucial to innovation.

Regulators should consider global implications. U.S. export control rules need to be precise and targeted, but not needlessly inhibiting to firms. Likewise, if a U.S. export order requires inspection by foreign buyers, visa regulations should flexibly accommodate the need for a brief visit.

But who pays for the adjustments? Currently, there is no link between governmental market openings and benefits obtained by an industry. Trade negotiations results in winners and losers, but winners have no incentive to share their bounty. The beneficiaries of protective measures do not show how they have used their revenues to help the transition of workers and communities. This must change. Private-sector winners must supplement the federal Trade Adjustment Assistance programs to help fund the cost of adjustment and become an essential engine for further trade liberalization. After all, even free trade has its price.

In Need of Honorable Merchants

Originally Published by the Sri Lanka Guardian: June 7, 2014

A powerful concept in today's international marketing field focuses on re-establishing honorable practices in the workplace and, more importantly, across borders.

The emphasis on the Honorable Merchant is a renewed issue in Europe, bringing fresh life to old thoughts. What exactly is an Honorable Merchant? It dates back at least to medieval history and ancient mercantile practices, where trust was paramount for achieving success. "Honorable practices" are rules established to guide merchants in conducting international business. For example, Berhold v. Regensburg admonished in 1210 that merchants should always use accurate measures and weights, highlighting Honorable practices as a priority in society. These rules go all the way back to Proverbs (11:1), which specifically address merchants: "A false balance is an abomination to the Lord, but a just weight is his delight." The New Testament, Matthew 19:23-24, cites Jesus as saying 'it is easier for a camel to go through the eye of a needle than for someone who is rich to enter the kingdom of God'. Later on, the Quran resolves that charging interest is inappropriate and even sinful (Quran 3:130-131). In Chinese society, the role of a merchant was seen as a necessary evil, far below more exalted societal roles, such as imperial officials.

Honor also implied accountability beyond the merchants themselves, extending to their leaders. In the early 15th century, creditors from abroad requested that citizens convince their nobility to pay their trade debts. If not, they threatened attack not only on the noblemen and cities themselves, but every merchant from those cities.

A summary then indicates:

The profession of merchants often has a dubious reputation, even more so internationally.

Mixed emotions are prevalent, since merchants can either help or hinder through their work.

Internationally, merchants may be at a disadvantage due to their foreignness. Their background and differences could detract from success in business.

International merchants are attractive since they bring choice to market, however they still may displace domestic relationships.

To overcome this psychic distance, merchants must compensate for their shortcomings.

Merchants have long faced a variety of objections, making it difficult to climb the path to trust. Trust can facilitate investments in relationship assets, encourage information sharing, and lower transaction costs. However, Honorable practices have developed over time, by building long-term customer relationships. We believe that the outcome of Honorable behavior will be the construction of Trust Bridges.

An Honorable Merchant's reputation can be developed by high-lighting commonalities and shared experiences, which establish a set of standards for international business. Exposing two parties to common conditions and values helps establish connectivity, warmth and trust more rapidly than if they had no similar experiences. Through a combination of collaboration, symposia, conferences, and courses, partners can accredit and certify people or companies through a database of Trust Bridges.

In its annual Global Marketing conference, held recently in Cancun, the American Marketing Association sought to help in developing the honorable merchant concept. Today's critical characteristics of an Honorable Merchant must be to 1) build trust, 2) demonstrate corporate social responsibility (CSR), and 3) offer integrity and reliability, i.e. just because something can be done, the Honorable Merchant will not necessarily do it. All this needs to occur simultaneously in the realms of academia, business, and policy.

An essential application of a Trust Bridge exists for alumni of a university. A university's ability to establish an extraordinary environment enables the building of common bridges, anchored in similar life experiences. The most effective way to develop strong relationships is to high-light what each party brings to the table. Team work, networking and reputation will increasingly become the main factor in choosing to attend a brick and mortar university, even after the web and internet provide alternatives to traditional education. However, for such efforts to be victorious, they must go beyond the mere transfer of information and help interested parties collaborate and connect.

Familiarity brings a fast track to relationships. A data base of shared experiences can be instrumental in fostering such familiarity. A greater capacity for trust is developed through understanding, which shapes honorable relationships. Honorable practices should again become the expectation and norm.

Great Chinese Ham from Virginia

(With Charles Skuba)

Originally Published in Ovi Magazine: June 21, 2013

For many Americans, Virginia ham is a long established part of a festive family dinner. But good old American traditions like that can carry new meaning in a global economy. The news that Smithfield Foods, owner of leading pork brands like Smithfield Ham, Eckrich sausages, Armour meatballs and Farmland bacon, is to be acquired by Chinese company Shuanghui International Holdings Ltd. caused indigestion for some in the United States.

The $4.7 billion deal, announced on May 30, 2013, would be the largest acquisition of a U.S. company by a Chinese firm. It is another of a series of recent significant global acquisitions by Chinese firms. Other examples include the 2012 purchase of the AMC movie chain by Dalian Wanda Group Corp. of Bejing and the 2013 acquisition, of Canada's Nexen by China National Offshore Oil Corporation (Cnooc). At year's mid-point, 2013 promises to be a record year for Chinese foreign direct investment in the United States. It is also indicative of a new focus for Chinese investment: branded consumer businesses. Previous investment attempts by Chinese companies have not always gone smoothly. A big obstacle has been that many deals have touched on national security sensitivity. The Committee on Foreign Investment in the United States (CFIUS), is a U.S. inter-agency government panel that reviews foreign deals for national security issues. It is doubtful that CFIUS will have concerns after the (consumer good based) Smithfield acquisition.

China may well be approaching a tipping point for an economic transition from being export focused to becoming consumption-driven. After improving the world by manufacturing good basic products, Chinese businesses must now learn how to succeed through marketing and excellence.

Marketing guru Philip Kotler defines marketing as both an art and a science. Chinese firms have mainly concentrated on science, via price. Now they must become better at creating higher quality products, placing them in distribution outlets that Western consumers prefer, and promoting them with a direct appeal to Western emotions. The best way to accomplish all this quickly is through the acquisition of Western firms with already established base of consumer preference. Therefore, in addition to the establishment of new brands, we are likely to see a significant expansion of Chinese acquisitions of U.S. and European consumer goods brands in the coming years.

Is this a good thing? Acquisitions by foreigners tend to be accompanied by concerns. When U.S. giant Kraft acquired British Cadbury, there was worry about diminished chocolate quality in the U.K. Now Americans (accompanied with much hamming it up by master comic Jay Leno) state that the Smithfield acquisition could lead to diminished quality and loss of American jobs.

Far from it ! The Chinese are not just obtaining products—imports and exports would have done that. Rather, the acquisition helps integrate China into the global economy, and contributes to its future branding success by delivering new connections, experience, capabilities and trust. The key benefits will be learning of both quality and marketing.

Of even more interest is the reverse flow, where international investments have a spillover effect on home country markets. Why not eat Hunan pork with Smithfield ham during a picnic at the Yangtze river? What pork other than Smithfield's should be specified when planning the Chinese government-subsidized opening of restaurant chains in Africa ? The Smithfield acquisition opens new markets both for the Chinese investors as well as for American ham. Such is the path of true globalization.

The emerging middle class in China represents enormous opportunity not only for Smithfield but also for many American companies. But, such market expansion must be a two-way street. For more American firms to be able to have access to the Chinese marketplace, Chinese firms must be allowed and encouraged to compete in the United States.

Surely US Set to Reconcile

Originally Published in the Japan Times: November 6, 2004

After a campaign that stressed the importance of continuity, some might expect few changes in policies during the second term of President George W. Bush. But the outcome of this bitterly fought election has clarified many issues in the United States and will send a signal far beyond America.

Many called this election the most important one in a generation. As the results show us, this claim was more than customary campaign rhetoric. If American voters had followed the traditional path of voting on their pocketbooks, the short-term economy and their jobs, then the

Kerry team would have been victorious. If money politics and the support of Hollywood stars had been decisive, again Mr. Kerry would have carried the day. But, contrary to many early tracking polls, the American public appears to have broken with expected traditions.

This election has shown that, to the U.S. electorate, moral principles matter. Call it dedication, commitment, a willingness to stand up for a cause—all these watchwords, which in many countries around the world have become so unpopular lately, have found a new appeal in the U.S. In how many other nations could a leader have prevailed with essentially a one-track mind focused on fighting terrorism?

Who would have thought that "blood, sweat and tears" could lead to victory in the new millennium? Was it serendipity or providence that the princes of the Catholic Church virtually endorsed the non-Catholic candidate on the Sunday before the election—and that there were enough of the faithful attending church to listen and to follow the appeal?

The largest number of voters ever has gone to the polls, demonstrating the high level of interest in this election. So now there is, for the first time in more than a decade, a president elected with the majority of the popular vote. He will be supported by a Senate that is more firmly, and more conservatively, in Republican hands and whose minority Democratic leader has lost re-election. The House of Representatives has increased its Republican majority as well. Yes, some changes can be expected.

On a domestic level, this victory makes it much easier for the president to reach out and unite the country. The winners know where they are headed and can afford to be magnanimous. The minority party will now be able to move beyond the disappointment of 2000 and accept the voter reality of 2004. Together, and without the constant party bickering of the past, the two parties can achieve great and necessary improvements for America.

On the international field, there will be an internal strengthening of the mandate for U.S. leadership—not just by might its throw-weight or technology but also by its having survived what was perhaps the heaviest onslaught of distortional campaigning in the country's history. There will be a willingness for a fresh start.

Here are a few of the cornerstones of the new policy field: Solutions are expected to come primarily from the private sector. Individual initiative, be it through entrepreneurship, collaboration or partnership, will be rated highly and encouraged. Public sector answers will likely take a back seat. Globally, this is a victory for enlightened self-interest.

In coping with the U.S. trade gap between exports and imports, this orientation is likely to encourage approaches that promote a steep increase in exports rather than a government-imposed decline in imports. There will likely be major efforts to provide for a level and open international playing field—which includes identifying and tearing down trade barriers followed by encouragement of U.S. firms to become players on a field where 95 percent of the potential participants are from outside the U.S. Of course, there are limits on the degree to which one can expect the U.S. to remain the unconditional and only champion of free trade. Every policy has its price—even if it has the word "free" associated with it.

The nexus of trade and foreign policy will be better recognized—perhaps even shades of a new Francophilia—leading to more resolute rewards for allies. If we can't help our friends, then who can we help may become a new watchword.

Global trade negotiations will be pursued in addition to many bilateral efforts to ease trade restrictions, and will not be unreasonably burdened by extraneous conditions and demands.

Investments from abroad are likely to be encouraged. Investment incentives are more likely to be workforce training or infrastructure investments rather than simple tax benefits. Outgoing investments and outsourcing activities are much less likely to be restricted than they would have been under a Kerry team, but tax support for investment abroad can not be expected.

Export controls will remain crucial. In an era where old alliances have entered a state of flux before new ones of long duration have been formed, a policy of reasonable caution can be expected. In his second term, Bush will be even less likely to listen to the siren song of merchant-driven desires at the expense of security—particularly when the proposals for the softening of controls come unilaterally from abroad.

This election may well mean the fracturing of more linkages at the tectonic-plate level between Europe and America. Ironically, it is the new world that is emerging as the conserver of old-fashioned values and a steadfast stick-to-itiveness that persists long after the polls have identified it as "inopportune."

Surely the administration is willing to reconcile and move forward, resolutely but with due caution. The many nonvoters around the world who so vociferously stated their opposition to the Bush administration should consider: Those whom the gods truly wish to punish get what they ask for. You have been spared!

The Rise of the Consumer
(With Charles Skuba)
Originally Published in Marketing Management—September/October 2009

Here we present more issues which will shape the future of marketing management in the changing global business environment. These are the latest findings from a study, using the Delphi method, in which senior executives from around the world rated key dimensions of the world economy that concern international marketing management. Our previous column identified terrorism, globalization and persistent corruption.

Now we address the demand side of global marketing and emerging trends in consumer behavior.

Rising Consumer Power

Consumers have provided the underpinning of global economic growth over the past two decades, as globalization has helped to spread prosperity over larger parts of the planet. Individual purchasing power has increased greatly as marketers have embraced the concept of customer as king. Consumers have remarkable influence on business decision making as marketers seek to learn more about their needs, wants, desires, dreams and frustrations. As companies look to Asia, Central and Eastern Europe, Russia, Latin and Central America and Africa for increasing shares of revenue growth, the need for reliable research data is critical. Marketers must carefully weigh the costs of adapting products and marketing them to these growing markets.

At the same time, real or feared job loss, depleted individual savings and shaken confidence have stunted consumer spending. One of the most striking lessons learned in the past year has been how closely the world economies are linked. As individual insecurity has risen, so has the role of governments. Many early seek dramatic solutions. Some in government look to import restrictions and "buy domestic" programs to keep home industries safe and to address global imbalances. In many of these approaches, the consumer may end up as the ultimate loser.

Consumer Behavior Issues

Whether the current crisis will persist or the "green shoots" of recovery are actually sprouting, one things is certain—the global consumer will be the ultimate source of recovery. Our experts offer some interesting insights about their expected behavior.

1. Cultural adjustment. Our study revealed a seeming dichotomy in regard to cultural assimilation. While there is a strong belief that cultures around the globe will become more similar to one another—particularly in macro issues such as accountability, performance expectations, freedom accorded within society and product preferences—there is also a perception that uniform ways of thinking, as influenced by the United States, will be less accepted due to increased assertion of regional and local idiosyncrasies and sovereignty.

   The key task for governments is to identify cultural conflicts early on, and to prevent them from becoming irreconcilable. There must be an ongoing search for ways to keep society cohesive, connected and ready for collaboration. Governments must understand the investment models driving the behavior of firms, and provide a platform that allows business to mitigate the sometimes harsh market dynamics created by high risk conditions. There is also a need to reconcile the benefits of corporate growth with consumer expectations for an increased role in the marketplace.

The corporate challenge is to take advantage of the opportunities of globalization, while reflecting unique cultural preferences, tastes and values. Asian tastes and preferences will increasingly influence product design and corporate business practices. Also, look for corporations to opt for more use of soft power (such as corporate philanthropy) in coping with local requirements in the global marketplace. A challenge fro the companies will be the increasing expectations of societies and governments related to the extent and nature of corporate social responsibility programs and practices. What was once voluntary is quickly becoming compulsory with sometimes retroactive enforcement—if not by law, then by sentiment.

2. Conservation and sustainability. Green gains global marketing muscle, as consumers exercise the power of demand in the environmental arena. In light of public concern about climate change, there will be a growing preference for energy-saving technologies and a reduction and limit to energy use. Public impressions and perceptions will lead to changes in living patterns and habits. Consumers will increasingly favor products and services from companies with strong sustainability practices.

While governments and companies adjust to both a stronger eco-consciousness and the realities affecting economic growth, there may emerge an uneven playing field.

In its drive to grow, China will demonstrate only limited concern toward the environment, even though environmental problems will have a major affect on its ability to compete as a global manufacturing center. At the same time, environmental, health and other social costs will dramatically reduce the advantages of firms to manufacture in China—with a resultant shift of investment.

A major consequence of China's and India's rapid growth will be an ongoing depletion of natural resources. Aspirations for economic progress and better lifestyles will cause shortages in vital commodities. In response, governments will often be sorely tempted to worship the false idols of protectionism, administrative shelter, subsidies and price controls. Food shortages will result in the attempt to put more land into grain production, which leads to downstream problems of water shortages and land exhaustion.

3. Information. As marketers seek local insights, local data will become even more essential. A greater diversification of information sources may typically provide for better knowledge evolution. But mergers, acquisitions, cost cutting or limited user willingness to pay will lead to fewer data sources offering increasingly similar data. Data users will demand more knowledge about the origin of information, in order to gauge its validity and trustworthiness.

Panelists also expect that there will be a decrease in the willingness of firms and people to offer information at no or low prices. Increased transparency requirements, along with laws and restrictions that raise the threat of law suits, will be coupled with a desire to participate in the financial benefits of knowledge transmissions.

Trade Barrier Importance

Although our experts predict that consumers will continue to exercise more muscle, the increasing role of governments in the marketplace will inevitably have both positive and negative consequences. With growing public anxieties over financial security and loss of domestic jobs, continued and increased protectionist policies may well result in decreased consumer options. The victims of these policies are not only global businesses but consumers as well. Whether it concerns Chinese families in need of banking services, American connoisseurs of Roquefort cheese, Europeans in need of a good American steak or Indian oenophiles, tariff and non-tariff barriers rob individuals of the opportunities to pursue product preferences. The commitment of governments to lowering trade barriers is key to a better life.

Our next article will address emerging economies, growth industries and demographic changes. We will further explore strategic requirements for success in light of these and other trends, as well as the need for reform in global marketing management.

SECTION 2

On Innovation in Today's Global Community

.

Achieving 'Glocal' Success
(With Ilkka A. Ronkainen)
Originally Published by the American Marketing Association: April 2014

Many of the most successful global companies have adopted an organizational approach that provides clear global strategic direction along with the flexibility to adapt to local opportunities and requirements. The term "glocal" has been coined to describe this approach. Big and small organizations have the scale and resources of a global powerhouse, but also the speed, creativity and agility of a fresh, new startup.

Companies that have adopted this approach have incorporated the following four dimensions into their organizations.

Building a Shared Vision

The first dimension relates to a clear and consistent long-term corporate mission that guides individuals wherever they work in the organization. Examples of this are Johnson & Johnson's corporate credo of customer focus; Coca-Cola's mission of leveraging global beverage brand leadership "to refresh the world, inspire moments of optimism and happiness, create value and make a difference"; Nestlé's vision to make the company the "reference for nutrition, health and wellness"; and Samsung's mission to "create superior products and services, thereby contributing to a better global society." But formulating and communicating a vision or mission cannot succeed unless individual employees understand and accept the company's stated goals and objectives.

Broadening Perspectives

This relates to the development of a cooperative mindset among region or country organizations to ensure the effective implementation of global strategies. Managers may believe that global strategies are intrusions on their operations if they do not have an understanding of the corporate vision, if they have not contributed to the global corporate agenda, if they are not given direct responsibility for its implementation or if there is no reward for their cooperation.

Also, negative attitudes towards certain "foreign activities" such as marketing can prevent management abroad from participating fully in the process of change. Defensive, territorial attitudes can lead to the emergence of the "not invented here" syndrome—that is, country organizations objecting to or even rejecting a sound strategy. Education and information play a major role in getting local managers on board with a strategy, and, more important yet, in letting them work accurately with others. It is much easier to be truthful with others when one understands the issues at hand, as well as the plans for the future.

For example, in an area structure, country units may operate quite independently. To tackle potential problems, firms conduct management meetings once a month to supervise regional operations. Each committee includes representatives of the major functions, such as manufacturing, marketing and finance. Yum Brands has a structure that emphasizes its individual brands, including KFC, Pizza Hut, Taco Bell and Long John Silver's, but it also has three operational units: one for the U.S. market, an international division and a separate China division covering mainland China, Thailand and KFC Taiwan because of the size and strategic importance of China.

The network avoids the problems of duplication of effort, inefficiency and resistance to ideas developed elsewhere by giving subsidiaries the latitude, encouragement and tools to pursue local business development within the framework of the global strategy. Headquarters considers each unit a source of ideas, skills, capabilities and knowledge that can be used for the benefit of the entire organization. This means that the subsidiaries must be upgraded from the role of implementation and adaptation to that of contribution and partnership in the development and execution of worldwide strategies. Efficient plants may be converted into international production centers, innovative R&D units may become centers of excellence (and thus role models), and key subsidiary groups may be given a leadership role in developing new strategic approaches for the entire corporation.

Allowing maximum flexibility at the country-market level takes advantage of the fact that subsidiary management knows its market and can react to changes quickly. Problems of motivation and acceptance are avoided when decision makers are also implementing the strategy. On the other hand, many marketers faced with global competitive threats and opportunities have adopted global strategy formulation, which, by definition, requires some degree of centralization. What has emerged as a result can be called "coordinated decentralization," which means that the overall corporate strategy is provided from global or regional headquarters, but subsidiaries are free to implement it within a range established in consultation between headquarters and the subsidiaries.

However, moving into this new mode may raise significant challenges. Among systemic difficulties is a lack of widespread commitment to dismantling traditional national structures, driven by an inadequate understanding of the larger, global forces at work. Some organizational initiatives, such as multicultural teams or corporate chat rooms, may be jeopardized by the fact that people do not have the necessary skills—the language ability, Six Sigma, etc.—or that an infrastructure such as an intranet may not exist in an appropriate format.

Capable Managers

The third component in the "glocal" approach is making use of representatives from different countries, regions, and cultures. Organizationally, the forces of globalization are changing the country manager's role significantly. With profit-and-loss responsibility, oversight of multiple functions, and the benefits (and drawbacks) of distance from headquarters, country managers enjoyed considerable decision-making autonomy, as well as entrepreneurial initiative. Today, however, many companies have to emphasize the product dimension of the product-geography matrix, which means that power has to shift at least to some extent from country managers to worldwide strategic business unit and product line managers. Many of the previously local decisions are now subordinated to global strategic moves.

However, regional and local brands still require an effective local management component. Therefore, the future country manager will have to have diverse skills, such as government relations and managing entrepreneurial teamwork, and wear many hats in balancing the needs of the operation for which the manager is directly responsible with those of the entire region or strategic business unit. To emphasize the importance of the global/regional dimension in the country manager's portfolio, many companies have tied the country manager's compensation to the way the company performs globally or regionally, not just in the market for which the manager is responsible.

The human factor in any organization is critical. Managers both at headquarters and in the subsidiaries must bridge the physical and psychic distances separating them. If subsidiaries have competent managers who rarely need to consult headquarters about conditions of overlaps and tradeoffs between units, they may be granted high degrees of autonomy. In the case of global organizations, subsidiary management must understand the corporate culture because subsidiaries must sometimes make decisions that meet the long-term objectives of the firm as a whole but that are not optimal for the local market.

Internal Cooperation

In today's environment, the global business entity can be successful only if it is able to move intellectual capital within the organization—that is, to transmit ideas and information in real time. If there are impediments to the free flow of information across organizational boundaries, important updates about changes in the competitive environment might not be communicated in a timely fashion to those tasked with incorporating them into the strategy.

For example, Procter & Gamble makes the recruitment and teaching of future leaders a priority for its top executives. All of the top officers at the company teach in the company's executive education programs, and act as mentors and coaches for younger managers. P&G takes global executive development seriously and grooms its top management prospects through a series of career-building assignments across business units and geographies. Eighty-five percent of the company's top management have had one or more international assignments.

WPP, the global marketing services group, has developed a graduate marketing fellowship program for promising global managers comprising three one-year rotations with individual companies within the group's global network and requiring an international assignment.

Another method to promote internal cooperation for global strategy implementation is the use of international teams or councils. In the case of a new product or program, an international team of managers may be assembled to develop a strategy. While final direction may come from headquarters, such direction will now be informed of local conditions. Implementation of the strategy is enhanced since local country managers were involved in its development.

This approach has worked even in cases involving seemingly impossible market differences. In some cases, it is important to bring in members of other constituencies—for example, suppliers, intermediaries or service providers—to such meetings to share their views and experiences, and make available their own best practices for benchmarking. In some major production undertakings, technology allows ongoing participation by numerous internal and external team members. The key is cooperation and joint value identification for the firm and its employees in order to leverage corporate capabilities and resources throughout all spans of the organization to achieve the best positive outcomes.

GM in Asian Auto Markets

(With Charles Skuba)

Originally Published in the Korea Times: June 14, 2009

The U.S. government now owns 60 percent of General Motors. Some say that the company really belongs to the taxpayers—but just have them try to sell some of "their" GM shares—they'll quickly see how limited their ownership rights are.

U.S. officials now have a new mandate that is familiar to business executives: meet increased sales goals in an ever-expanding sales territory. If GM is to succeed, global sales and operations, not just American, must be a priority.

In an industry that is among the most competitive in the world, GM's future will inevitably be linked to global markets and how well it does as an Asian car company.

Of course, this is not lost on GM. Indeed, at the same time as the firm filed for Chapter 11 protection, CEO Fritz Henderson said that "China remains a key part of our business. Our ventures in China are a critical part of the new GM—unequivocally. Our business in China continues to grow at a very fast, even torrid pace and remains a critical part of GM going forward."

As GM pares down its presence in Europe with the sales of Opel and Saab, the company has expansive ambitions in Asia.

China is GM's largest growth market. The firm has more than 20,000 employees, enjoys booming sales and occupies the leading position among global automakers with market share of about 12 percent in the region.

GM has numerous Chinese joint ventures including major deals with Shanghai Automotive (SAIC) and Wuling to sell Chevrolet, Buick and Cadillac as well as Wuling-brand light commercial vehicles. The *China Daily* reported that GM plans to open a new factory and double sales in China over the next five years.

Another significant Asian market for the new GM will be South Korea, where it is the majority owner of GM Daewoo Auto & Technology, Korea's third largest automaker.

While GM Daewoo has struggled with the global downturn in auto sales and is seeking support from the Korea Development Bank, GM executives have stated that the company plans to expand its GM Korean operations.

Elsewhere in Asia, auto markets have been more depressed by the economic crisis, yet GM plans for growth throughout the region with emphasis on Thailand and India. In fact, GM is seeking local financing in Southeast Asia to expand operations.

In India, look for GM to engage Tata's Nano in competition with its own version of a mini car. India should be a hot market as the country continues its strong economic growth.

With 95 percent of the world's customers living outside the United States, GM must look overseas for long-term expansion.

The new GM ad campaign promises that "GM gets down to business" with the "rebirth of the American car." But this rebirth better be with Asian consumers in mind.

As GM searches for innovations in the small car market, Korea, China and India will be the most logical sources of cutting-edge products.

GM's long-term success in Asia, and perhaps globally, will likely come from four-cylinder, fuel-efficient cars developed by GM Daewoo or in China at GM's Pan Asia Technical Automotive Centre (PATAC) joint venture with SAIC.

The growing needs of Asian markets will require adjustments in production capacity and product. Consistent with the product cycle theory, over time, established products are produced in new locations with more local advantages.

Asian production sites with lower cost structures and locally based R&D are essential for the new GM to fulfill its mission. To succeed in its post-bankruptcy life, GM will need to rationalize its global production platform to maximize economies of scale and eliminate waste.

While GM will need to temper its ambitions to avoid mistakes of the past, it must compete globally or be marginalized as a niche competitor. However, global efficiency becomes particularly sensitive if GM uses overseas production facilities to import cars to the United States.

Indeed, the U.S. administration's rescue plan for GM is contingent upon producing more cars in the United States, even as it closes factories and eliminates jobs at home.

Yet, inefficient production is one of the principal reasons for GM's Chapter 11 filing and should not be championed under the guise of protecting American jobs.

Utah Gov. Jon M. Huntsman, the designated U.S. ambassador to China, has his work cut out. He will be confronted with competitive realism while supporting American idealism. But he's the right man for a tough job.

The Obama administration may not intend to be an active manager of the new GM but its policies on trade, foreign investment and taxation will shape the company's future.

Government policies must allow and even encourage GM to be competitive not just at home, but also abroad. Don't expect administration officials to go on commission, but, whether they like it or not, they have a new obligation to help GM increase sales. Asia is the smart place to look.

What We Should Be Teaching Our Kids That Isn't Found in Heavy Bookbags

(With Thomas A. Czinkota)

Orginally Published in the Shanghai Daily: November 2, 2009

There is no doubt that children today are being overworked and over-scheduled—but do the Czinkota brothers have a good point about what education should be?

WE just concluded the fall school vacation. Between us two brothers, we have three children, 6, 7, and 10, with whom we spent the week in conversation, playing and thinking.

Here are some of the issues that we considered, but are not sure that we solved:

Are children overworked?

Over time growing societal surpluses have made it possible to enjoy the fruits of our labors. We no longer learn only because we have to, but because we want to and we can focus on learning about history and enjoyment of art, music and poetry, about beauty.

Even though the need for learning has changed, the process and conditions of learning have not been altered to provide for a more relaxed childhood.

Kids are increasingly over-scheduled little beasts of burden with more work of greater complexity carried in ever heavier knapsacks on wheels.

The available knowledge has increased greatly.

Yet, our children keep on learning the way their parents did. Are we perhaps maintaining an outdated approach, applying it to vastly increased quantities of content with a greatly diminished half-life ?

Memory outdated?

Could it be that all we are doing is cramming our children's brains with more useless stuff?

We exert pressure on our children so that they learn.

Just as high pressure can transform coal into diamonds, perhaps our children grow more talented. We punish them for not doing sufficient work. Boredom is no excuse. Of course, shouldn't we ask why the same child is not getting bored by TV shows, discussions with friends, or playing with dolls?

In a pharmacological society, many kids are given prescription pills to cure what once was seen as typical (highly active) child behavior. We have even seen children who have their own personal assistant charged with keeping them focused.

But there are also procedural learning questions: Why do children still memorize?

Memorization had its origins when there was no print, no dictionaries, and therefore no institutional retention. Priests and monks had to memorize in order to pass on society's knowledge—they were the living word.

Today, we have Google, we have Bing, we have Wikipedia; all systems that remember things for us. Of course, it is said that by subscribing to Wikipedia we are buying into the hidden agenda of secretive editors. Well, why not? For centuries we've bought into the hidden agendas of the secretive editors of the Oxford Dictionary. Even the monks and scribes who laboriously produced manuscripts, added or eliminated details. So the flexibility and adjustment of materials has a long tradition.

Alternatives

How much knowledge does a child realistically need?

Will (or should) the acquired knowledge ever be useful for anything? Does it make sense to dispense knowledge in a shotgun approach (we give you everything and hope some of it helps)?

There is always a great reluctance to move away from existing patterns. There used to be a firm conviction that only the slide rule would maintain the algebraic memories of children.

After our vacation together, we ask ourselves whether it isn't much more important to spend time with our children to play more, listen to and perform more music, exercise in more sports, engage in more theater productions?

We need to explain to them the things they need to know—for example about morals, values, a sense of excitement and pleasure; about the facts of life, that prices are typically not the result of costs but of demand and supply; about friendship, and the enjoyment and benefits of new people networks.

With such knowledge our children might not be able to avoid a global trade and financial crisis, but at least they will understand it and react to it.

International Marketing: An Imperative for Southeast Europe

(With Valbona Zeneli)

Originally Published by George C. Marshall European Center for Security Studies: January 2014

The science of international marketing is new to Southeast Europe (SEE), though this year marks the 75th anniversary of the nascence of this academic field. Marketing has shifted over time from a strictly domestic focus to globalization, linking all the markets together. Recent crises and recessions in the world have slowed down the very fast pace of globalization of the recent two decades and has also reduced the global penetration of international investment. Most crucial at this time is the fact that reductions in trade and investment flows are not just a matter of money and finance, but rather of policy and trust.

Under the aegis of industrial policies, a growing number of countries have introduced new non-tariff barriers and hidden restrictions to trade and investments, adding an actual interventionist approach to globalization, and leading—directly or indirectly—to inhibitions in internationalization and a rise in protectionism.

Policy makers, non-governmental organizations, businesses and consumers have become more selective about whom they trade with or buy from, how much access they want to give to foreign investors, and what sort of capital they invest and admit.

One needs to acknowledge that only two decades ago, today's new reality was not addressed or even anticipated by most market forces or marketing sages. Today, we are again in a similar position: There is now a newly emerging direction of marketing focused on restoring trust and coaxing development through new tools synchronized with international economic health. Drawing lessons from the crises early in this new century, the new generation of marketers, whether in their old market places or in the era and areas of new opportunities, should address the necessity of overall welfare and inclusive development. International economic cooperation and integration have become imperative, if one is to meet the new global challenges.

Why international marketing in Southeast Europe (SEE)?

In the small region of SEE, marketing is mainly seen to be about the domestic market, and only for business executives. It is not even considered an important part of government strategy for development. However, we believe that a small market size requires both firms and governments to stride beyond their traditional confines, giving them new perspectives, and new forms of doing business. Hence, international marketing is important for businesses and governments and individuals.

Similarly, inbound international marketers have shown little interest in this small region. SEE has therefore arrived at an image characterized by a history of conflicts, wars, regional disputes and mistrust among neighbors, accompanied by high levels of organized crime and corruption. Though Southeast Europe offers unique opportunities in terms of strategic position, natural resources, relatively cheap labor, and youth of population, it still attracts very little serious foreign direct investment (FDI). In light of recent economic crises which have re-boosted the role of the governments in the economy, it is time for the governments of SEE to understand the benefits coming from international marketing and make the activity a top priority.

Freedom

International marketing is a notion of freedom, which removes boundaries between nations and grants more choices to citizens. It offers broad opportunities. The notion of freedom is particularly important for the former socialist countries of SEE. After their market conversion all regional countries embraced free trade regimes, liberalized their economies, and took on membership in the WTO. However, the culture of international economic cooperation and the linkage effects of interdependence are new phenomena for these economies.

Opportunity and Contentment

International marketing is the best way to increase national strength and status for nations of limited territory and resources. This key activity strengthens both individuals and nations. The countries of SEE are small and inexperienced in international business competition. They lack resources: financial, technological, and knowhow and products. Only by engaging in the international market, will companies gain the necessary skills still amiss. Also, when decisions are made on a one country one vote basis, as in the World Trade Organization every country is somewhat the same size.

Prosperity and Innovation

International marketing rewards excellence. It augurs more quality and enhances standards of living. Due to international marketing, many countries have, within the last two decades, significantly increased their standards of living and wealth. Market allocations typically result in more options and a better utilization of skills than was achieved through government fiat, leveraging a nation's capabilities and resources which already exist and offering more opportunities to improve.

International marketing gives hope by offering better job prospects and improved skills. Hence, governments should engage in creating a business environment friendly to quality FDI in strategic sectors and repugnant of rampant corruption. It is the quality and performance of institutions what worries investors the most when they consider entering a new foreign market.

Culture

International marketing helps us to better understand our fellow human beings. It will be easier to accept cultural differences, adapt (to) them, and benefit from a much broader perspective. In SEE this is particularly important, considering the cultural diversity of the Balkan region and the historically difficult relations between countries.

Markets themselves are a form of democracy. Corporate networks and multinational firms develop also efficiency based frameworks. Among the indirect positive effects of FDI in the host market are the organization's behavior and the adherence to corporate responsibility standards. To obtain the benefits of international marketing, political stability and economic reforms are crucial.

Way Ahead for Southeast Europe

By adopting an international marketing perspective, SEE will also need to make choices regarding the four critical pillars whose use and acceptance lead to globalization success. These are competition, risk, profit, and retention of ownership. In today's diverse societies, there is no uniformity of thought regarding the steps acceptable for success in the international market. The business world today recognizes the precariousness of its victory of economic progress. The vanquishment of others does not assure their acceptance of one's own fundamental tenets. There can be resentment, envy and even expectations of free resources, all accompanied by very little willingness to engage oneself. It is therefore not just altruism but also a quite enlightened self interest which lets nations at a high level of economic performance encourage and support the acceptance of international marketing by nations of less wealth. Such acceptance helps not only create a buffer zone against economic adversaries, but also encourages global support for existing business practices. However, time is of essence.

SECTION 3

On Daily Life and International Affairs

Economic Lessons from the Olympics

(With Jiashin Cui)

Originally Published by the Gulf Daily News—August 8, 2012

As the Olympics deliver another sports highlight to the world, some Americans remain highly irate with the uniforms worn by the U.S. team.

The reason: the team uniforms are made in China. One senior U.S. senator suggested piling up the uniforms and burning them. Some are even trying to use this controversy against presidential candidate Mitt Romney, due to his leadership of the 2002 Winter Olympics.

In response to this public relations debacle, Ralph Lauren, a design icon in the U.S., has already firmly committed that uniform production for the 2014 Winter Olympic game will take place on U.S. soil. Before we sweep this controversy under the rug, however, here are a few thoughts on the importance of the Olympics for economic thinking.

First off, there are also others who voice discontent about their national Olympic outfits. The British public, host of the games, complains about its uniforms designed by Stella MaCartney. They believe that there is not enough red in the uniforms, which therefore do not seem to sufficiently reflect the national colors of the U.K.

Second, it almost seems as if the debate over the labels on the uniforms draws more attention than the actual preparation of team USA or the London games themselves. Shouldn't the essence of the Olympics lie in the performance of the athletes from around the world competing with each other to excel by fulfilling the Olympic motto: "Citius, Altius, Fortius" (Faster, Higher, and Stronger).

There is no part of the motto calling for "domesticus" or "pulcher." One could well argue that attention should mainly be focused on the performance of the athletes, rather than how they look during the opening ceremony. Furthermore, the real performance is not delivered in dress uniforms, but rather in the swimsuits or leotards made wet and sweaty by competition.

If there were to be a debate, the quality of the uniforms rather than the source of production should receive public attention. The Olympics are all about effectiveness and efficiency. The economic argument should focus on a cost benefit analysis of those uniforms.

Does the outsourcing of stitching tasks to China lower the costs, and how does such international procurement affect quality? There is no need for a patriotic argument here, but rather the simple exploration of whether the team gets what has been paid for. If there has to be some flag waiving about Olympic clothes, then it might be during the entrance of the Chinese team, since its national basketball team and six other Chinese sports teams will compete in outfits featuring the swoosh of Nike, a U.S. owned-brand.

The current debate over the Olympic clothes reflects much bigger issues such as the upcoming U.S. presidential campaign and the subsequent formulation of national policy, but also the future direction of all major economies around the world. How should people deal with and respond to international competition both in terms of process and activity?

We all like to win, but the Olympics indicate that we should be willing to let everyone put up their best efforts and honor the highest performers. Typically, we prefer that participants on national teams are domestic citizens. But for special athletes (or products), outsourcing seems to be acceptable, yet touches a nerve if domestic conditions are problematic.

Comments made by some politicians about the Olympics and about the economy may sound silly and outrageous; but just like other outsourcing kerfuffles in the past, their true meaning ought to be taken with a grain of salt, and seen as the vote catching lamentations which they are. For both an economy and the Olympics, it seems unlikely that thoughtful leaders would ignore the value of designs and innovations in favor of low-value added sewing and stitching.

Super Bowl vs. Olympics: Discerning the Marketing Difference

(With Charles Skuba)

Originally Published By Ovi Magazine—January 24, 2014

Although the Super Bowl does reach viewers around the world, Olympic advertisers will be communicating with a much broader audience from diverse cultures who will bring with them a different set of interests and emotions. To persuade such a multicultural audience, advertising will need to seek commonalities of the mind and heart. Global advertising agencies have the expertise to create messages that work across borders and avoid the danger of leaving broad groups of viewers bewildered or, worse, offended.

We offer five winning techniques (not exclusive to each other) for creative messaging to global audiences during the Olympics in national and global media campaigns.

Universal Human Emotions

The best brands inspire and capture positive, if not joyful, emotion in their customers. Marketers know that emotion often trumps reason in purchase decisions. Dig deep into any customer psyche, whether of a business decision-maker or a teenage gamer, and you'll find a bundle of emotions that are common to people across cultures. Although there are cultural differences in what stirs emotion, some things are universal, like love stories and the pursuit of dreams.

For the 2012 London Olympic Games, P&G launched the global "Thank You Mom" campaign that celebrated the love of young Olympic athletes and their mothers. There may be no more powerful bond than the love between a mom and her child and that love is a universal emotion. Whenever we show the campaign film in class, it's guaranteed to start tears flowing. And, P&G's "Thank You Mom app" that allows people to thank their own moms crosses cultural boundaries.

http://news.pg.com/blog/thank-you-mom/procter-gamble-launches-global-thank-you-mom-campaign

Expansive Imagery

The film industry has conditioned viewers across the world to crave dramatic, expansive imagery. The most successful global films create a powerful impact in sight and sound. The Avengers amaze and inspire audiences globally with their technological and artistic power. The Olympics are a key opportunity for grand imagery.

Marketers regularly use striking visuals to capture attention but the bar is being raised. A dramatic recent marketing event was the Red Bull

Stratos mission and the awe-inspiring free fall jump of Felix Baumgartner from his stratospheric balloon. Millions of people around the world have seen the video and Red Bull continues to reap global benefits from the event.

http://www.redbullstratos.com/

Inspiring Sounds and Music

Hand-in-hand with expansive imagery are sounds and music. Music enhances visuals for dramatic and emotional impact. Marketers must be careful with music selection.

Coca Cola has long used "happiness" music to appeal to young people around the world. Coca Cola's use of music and visuals in David Corey's "The World of Ours" song for the 2014 FIFA World Cup in Brazil builds from the joyful 2010 campaign song, K'Naaan's "Wavin' Flag". Naturally, if the music is great, people will want to share it. Coca Cola, Facebook, and Spotify created a partnership to allow people around the world with access to Coca Cola's campaign music.

http://www.coca-colacompany.com/videos/coca-cola-placelists-bc2474722116001

Symbolism

If you want simple communication of an idea, it's hard to beat symbolism. IBM employs symbolism to enhance and distinguish its campaign and product messaging in its "Smarter Planet" campaign

https://www-304.ibm.com/partnerworld/wps/servlet/ContentHandler/pw_sol_smp_smarter-planet

Product Demonstration or Problem/Solution

If you can show product advantage in advertising, it's hard-working marketing. The trick is to get people's attention to your message. Samsung built in product demonstration for its Galaxy SII throughout its London 2012 Olympics advertising after getting attention through David Beckham's wringing a gong with a well-placed kick.

http://www.samsung.com/global/galaxys3/media.html

Also, marketers would be smart to walk away from messaging that depends upon slang or references to national pop culture. If you didn't grow up watching American television, you might not get a lot of pop culture references that U.S. audiences instantly understand.

The advertising that audiences will see during the upcoming Super Bowl will be uniquely tuned to American audiences while that of the Olympics will be globally focused. We are confident that both will employ many of the techniques identified here. Marketers are literally going for the global gold. For the audience, the Olympic marketing messages will be quite different from the ones of the Super Bowl but well worth waiting for.

The Kindest Cut: Pursuit of Prosperity Will Heal International Rifts

Originally Published by the Washington Times—March 26, 2003

"Fog over Channel, Continent cut off" is a newspaper headline attributed to the Times of London in the days of Empire. Today's fog of war again raises the specter of isolation this time juxtaposing the United States with parts of Europe.

The United States has entered the conflict with Iraq without the backing of some traditional players in world politics. Once the war is over, one can expect this reluctance to provide support to disappear quickly. Governments will be eager to forget the material and commercial support they gave to Iraq. They will want contracts for rebuilding the Middle East. Reaping the benefits from U.S. success without any of the risks is the classic syndrome of a free rider. Even though there are enough of them to fill the bus, if history is a guide, the United States will quickly return to friendship with people, but perhaps not with some governments.

Since the signing of the Treaty of Versailles in 1919, the United States has helped out and provided resources when it came to resolving difficulties abroad. This selflessness towards theworld continues to benefit countries ranging from Afghanistan to Zimbabwe. Americans and their policymakers tend to trust in the good of other people and believe that others are not that different from themselves. In cases of aggression, America has often been slow to respond. Typically, there is an eventual effort to right wrongs on a broad scale. Afterwards, Americans are quick to again be friends, build for a new future and move their lives and the lives of thevanquished forward. Think about it: How many superpowers planned their wars to minimize civilian casualties and damage to historic structures? How many prepared for reconstruction before the first soldier was engaged?

The trade dimension is the most amazing of all. With all the international machinations, theU.S. market remains a wide-open place for imports. There has been some highly publicized renaming of "French" foods on Capitol Hill. But legislation has not eliminated the inflow of French champagne and perfumes or German cars. On the contrary, the United States continues to offer its own market and consumptive power as an economic locomotive to theworld.

Critics abroad should think beyond the more than 10,000 jobs that are related to each $1 billion they export to the United States. They should look at the tremendous advances in technology, medicine, business processes and education and their dissemination around the globe, whichthe United States has made possible. They should think of the progress made in improving themasses' well-being. They should look at a key common thread the reasonable expectation of personal independence and self-reliance, supported by a public infrastructure which encourages progress. Innovation, creativity and improvements in processes and thinking are the hallmark of the United States and are shared with the world. The ability of individuals to create wealth and the rule of law to retain it is at an unprecedented high. For many individuals, this is the first time that they can think about playing offense rather than just defense!

At the same time, enlarging fissures have become evident in Europe. Still driven by many old rules and policies, by plans that are based on warm feelings and hopes rather than on facts, it seems increasingly rare that one hears a common European voice. The economic outlook may be from up high, but it looks into a hazy abyss. The freedom from the common threat of communism, which had sustained an alliance for almost half a century, has resulted in a weakening of the common bonds felt by some politicians. But it has not eliminated the relationships, the closeness and the indebtedness felt by individuals. Many of them greatly value past progress and future collaboration.

It is not countries but only some politicians who have cut themselves off from the United States, and they may find it an onerous and perhaps even embarrassing burden to reverse course. Their vehement utterances only reflect their inability to truly exert influence and their need to bask in a short-lived spotlight. All this does not obscure the efforts of the United States to reach a new plateau of prosperity and happiness. It is these pursuits which will heal the wounds of separation.

Royal Wedding: Tying US–UK Knot

(With Mariele Marki)

Originally Published in the Korea Times—February 5, 2011

On Friday, the royal wedding of Prince William of England and Kate Middleton took place. Hundreds of million of viewers around the world had their eyes glued to television units transmitting the momentous event.

If student action at Georgetown University is an indicator, in the U.S. at three in the morning, many Americans tuned in to live coverage of the royal wedding. Most major media networks were broadcasting from London.

According to a study by Nielsen, a leader in market research, "United States news and media outlets have out-published their U.K. counterparts in terms of wedding coverage."

The fascination and romanticism that the United States has for the royal family and the increase in attention ever since the engagement was announced last November, demonstrates the strong ties between the United States and the United Kingdom.

This cultural connection is an excellent example of a concept developed in international business. Psychological distance is the perceived distance from a firm to a foreign market, caused by cultural variables, legal factors, history and other societal norms.

A common model used to demonstrate this theory is a comparison of the link between the United States and Canada, and the United States and Mexico.

Americans tend to identify more with Canada than with Mexico. Both countries border the United States, but for reasons of language and culture, Canada appears to be psychologically much closer.

While the U.S. and the U.K. share the same language and have a linked history, one can also see the allure of royalty in both cultures.

Disney princesses have a strong presence in every young girl's childhood in the United States and many movies center around the plot of a fairytale with the prince and princess living happily ever after.

Women want to be treated like princesses and it is culturally very common to rejoice when one has "found her prince." Even though the U.S. hasn't had a royal leader in centuries, news on royal families is a regular part of television and magazine entertainment.

A large portion of the American population maintains a high level of interest in all that is regal.

Psychological proximity is much preferable to psychological distance. It helps business, creates friendships and leads to national decisions which are often unabashedly in favor of one's friends.

Psychological distance in turn tends to slow down relationships and, in a proverb mentioned by international travelers, affects the quality of the water one might otherwise share. That makes it important that all nations work on bridging distances through collaboration, mutual visits, and confidence-building measures.

Every business transaction is another step in mutual diplomacy which links nations together. Some nations even built their growth and success based on tying the knot and closing the distance.

For example, for centuries, the proverb in Europe was "Tu Felix Austria, nube," meaning that (in order to prosper,) you, lucky Austria, just get married.

However, as international business theory shows us, the best quality of psychological proximity occurs when it is close but not too close. Closeness creates better relationships and does make it easier for firms to enter markets.

But too much of a focus on similarities can lead to what may be considered unwelcome intrusiveness, and lets managers lose sight of important differences.

Even between the U.S. and the U.K. there are behavioral and language differences which are ignored at great peril. Just think of how new acquaintances address each other or how one talks about past accomplishments.

The fact that England still has a royal family and a society quite different from the U.S. makes the wedding interesting.

But interest does not mean that Americans would want to have royalty at home. Actually, many Americans would quite resent attempts to crown a domestic king. But that is discussed best over a spot of tea.

SECTION 4

On Business and Conflict

Terrorism and International Business

By Gary Knight and Gabriele Suder

Originally published in Japan Today— September 8, 2011

The airplanes of 9/11 forced countless multinational corporations (MNCs) to update their strategic planning. Our work with executives at more than 150 MNCs shows that 10 years later, companies are still grappling with how best to manage the terrorist threat.

In the two decades before 2001, the rate at which firms launched international ventures was growing rapidly. After 9/11, foreign direct investment fell dramatically as firms withdrew to their home markets.

The popularity of international-sounding company and brand names decreased appreciably as managers now emphasize domestic and local affiliations.

The tendency to reverse course on globalization has been accompanied by declining international education in the United States, as revealed by falling enrollments in foreign language and international business courses. In the past decade, managers shifted much of their focus from proactive exploration of international opportunities to a defensive posture emphasizing threats and vulnerable foreign operations.

In Europe, the radicalization of individuals and groups, motivated by ideology, religion or economic concerns, threatens local cooperation and social harmony. European business schools have benefited from tighter restrictions on international student enrollments in the U.S., but the focus of teaching has shifted from global to regional trade.

Another outcome of the terrorism threats has been a rise of public-private partnerships, in which governments and firms collaborate to counter them. For example, global police agencies now partner regularly with private firms to combat cyber crime and attacks on critical computer infrastructure.

Governments and activist groups now use social media to organize campaigns fighting against threats ranging from dictators to disease. But nations also have begun to curtail social media when they are contrary to government interests.

The cost of protecting against terrorism is many billions, while terrorist spend millions or less on their actions. There are abundant opportunities for small groups to employ non-weapon technologies, such as aircraft, to cause massive harm.

Though our capacity to protect key facilities has improved over time, the security focus on high-value assets encourages terrorists to redirect their violence at "soft targets" such as transportation systems and business facilities. Greater security at home means attacks will increasingly take aim on firms' foreign operations.

Companies have placed more emphasis on terrorism risk considerations when choosing how to enter foreign markets. In the last century, foreign direct investment (FDI) was the preferred approach. But terrorism has shifted the balance.

Now many more firms favor entry through exporting, which permits broad and rapid coverage of world markets, reduces dependence on highly visible physical facilities, and offers much flexibility for making rapid adjustments.

In terms of economies of scale and transaction costs, FDI is generally superior, but the risks of exporting are judged to be lower. Markets tend to punish failure more harshly than they reward success, which makes risk-minimizing strategies more effective.

Skillful management of global logistics and supply chains cuts the risk and cost of downtime. Firms seek closer relations with suppliers and clients in order to develop more trust and commitment. Some have increased "on-shoring" by bringing suppliers back into the country when their remoteness constitutes risk.

Terrorism causes an organizational crisis whose ultimate effects may be unknown, and poses a significant threat to the performance of the firm. Corporate preparedness for the unexpected is a vital task. Innovative managers develop back-up resources, and plan for dislocations and sudden shocks with a flexible corporate response.

Terrorism is a public threat, and some managers believe government should bear the cost of protecting against it. Others argue that a public-private partnership is the most effective approach, with firms taking the lead.

There is also the issue whether corporate headquarters or the locally exposed subsidiary should fund prevention and preparation expenditures. Regardless of who pays, everyone can agree on the need to guard against terrorism.

Every world region is vulnerable, and most attacks are directed at businesses and business-related infrastructure. Terrorism requires decision-making and behaviors that support vigilance and development of appropriate strategies. Managers who fail to prepare run the risk of weaker performance or even loss of the firm.

While we can no longer choose the lowest cost option, 10 years after 9/11 companies are more aware, less exposed, and less vulnerable to the risk of terrorism. But in the next 10 years comes the really big task: What can and should we do collectively and individually to reduce the causes of terrorism.

Afghanistan and War Against Terror

(With Gary Knight and Gabriele Suder)

Originally Published in the Korea Times—October 4, 2011

The "War on Terror" was launched 10 years ago, on Oct. 7, 2001. It represents a battle against terrorism, extremism and global geopolitical adversity seen to oppose democracy and freedom of choice.

In the intervening years, however, the war has produced various unintended consequences that threaten personal freedom and other liberties enjoyed by progressive societies worldwide.

Stringent inspections delay cargo and personnel at border crossings. In many cities, cameras constantly monitor the movement of vehicles and civilians alike.

Government wiretapping and surveillance procedures have been expanded. Bank transactions are scrutinized as never before. Airport security measures are annoying and sometimes even humiliating. In many ways, such intrusions represent a victory for terrorists.

An early casualty of the War on Terror was Afghanistan. During much of the time since October 2001, Afghans have seen little improvement in their lives and business conditions.

Ten years on, Foreign Policy labels Afghanistan a "failed state," especially regarding security, refugees, and legitimacy of the state. As the United States prepares an acceptable exit strategy, Afghanistan faces much risk and uncertainty.

Divided by religious and political strife, the country's per-capita income remains among the lowest worldwide. Adult literacy is below 28 percent and infant mortality is high. Following 30 years of war, Afghanistan's social, institutional, and commercial infrastructures are in a decrepit state.

The World Bank and World Trade Organization (WTO) have pointed to constraints that discourage corporate investment in Afghanistan: crime and disorder, inadequate energy and transport systems, and insufficient access to finance.

However, experts also suggest that, with appropriate local knowledge and collaborative efforts, companies can succeed in Afghanistan.

Success requires investments in education and training, creation of networks and infrastructure, and open-mindedness and flexibility toward the unexpected. Firms with significant experience in troubled regions are most likely to succeed.

Recent changes in Afghanistan have produced significant potential opportunities for early investors, especially in infrastructure development. The World Bank views Afghanistan as a prospective hub for regional trade.

The WTO points to significant improvements in the categories of "getting credit" and "registering property." Thanks to a modern secured transactions law that helps companies obtain loans, Afghanistan is now well ranked for "starting a business."

Afghanistan's economy is improving, especially in agriculture, commodities, and traditional industries. The nation is home to a wealth of natural resources, including natural gas, petroleum, and certain key minerals. It has benefited from billions of dollars of international aid and investments. In many ways, Afghanistan is typical of troubled regions around the world.

Experience with Afghanistan and the War on Terror has provided important lessons for Western governments and businesses alike. Companies now include terrorism as an important factor in their international planning.

Firms are devising international strategies that emphasize flexibility and the ability to change course quickly, with less dependence on vulnerable physical facilities.

Foresight and skillful management reduce the risk of loss and downtime. Companies are putting more emphasis on developing closer relations with governments and other key players in uncertain foreign markets.

Since the launch of the War on Terror, many world regions have experienced attacks and conflict. But companies are fighting back. Experienced managers are vigilant and favor approaches that ensure long-term, sustainable success.

Simultaneously, governments are learning to strike the right balance between security and unneeded intrusions in business and our personal lives.

Educators like us have an important role to play. Alongside managers and public authorities, we share a responsibility to redefine global commerce.

Increasingly, business must emphasize attitudes and behaviors that are not just ethical, but also socially responsible, compassionate, and focused on the long-term stability of nations worldwide.

Perhaps the best hope for a brighter future in troubled regions is business that, in addition to expanding profits, meets the social and economic needs of local stakeholders.

The struggle against terror, extremism and adversity is a long-term effort. The costs in human and financial terms are extremely important.

But hope remains eternal. Responsible, collaborative business can go far toward improving the social, political and economic landscape worldwide.

The global business community has both the capacity and responsibility to protect against the terrorist threat and to support development of a more sustainable, peaceful world.

On the Front Line: Marketers Combat Global Terrorism

Originally Published by Marketing Management May–June 2005

Marketers can be part of the solution in combating global terrorism.

Terrorism has existed for thousands of years, yet its global impact has changed significantly. Terrorism, which we define as "the threat or actual use of violence against civilians to attain a political goal through fear, coercion, or intimidation" now carries a sense of ubiquity and randomness we've never before experienced. Global mass media have ensured the unprecedented visibility and visualization of terrorist events, bringing fear to the world and creating an irrational expectation of localized attacks. Rising terrorism in Western nations adds a sense of immediacy, nearness, and urgency in countries previously considered immune. As a result, terrorists have had an impact far beyond their own expectations. Their "scores" include a decline of the global economy and the long-term depression of entire industries--such as aviation, retailing, and tourism.

Most managers, however, are ambivalent in their preparations for contingencies and new dangers. For most firms, the costs of averting terrorism are hard to quantify and even harder to justify to key stakeholders. In an era when spending mandates of the Sarbanes-Oxley legislation are straining corporate budgets, top executives put a greater premium on meeting financial performance benchmarks than on addressing hard-to-quantify risks.

According to the Council on Foreign Relations, in a 2002 report entitled "America Still Unprepared--America Still in Danger," most of the firms in the World Trade Center were caught off guard without terrorism contingency plans in both the 1993 attack and the Sept. 11, 2001 (9/11). Even today, most businesses are unprepared to meet the terrorist threat, and decision makers remain indifferent. CIO Insight, 2002, a survey of 337 executives, found that in the year following 9/11, spending on business continuity activities had not substantially increased. In his 2003 Business Insurance article, "Crisis Plan Key to Terror Safety," Mark Hofmann reports that figures from the world's largest insurance provider, Marsh Inc., show that only half of the Fortune 1,000 companies were looking to update their crisis management plans after 9/11. We believe that, particularly for marketing managers, such ignorance and apathy is unwise. In a volatile world, marketing operations are on the front line of risk--but marketing managers are not helpless.

No Immunity

During the past several years, we have formed a research team on various continents to study terrorism and its impact on business. To participate, see the questionnaire at http://msb. georgetown.edu/survey/terror.

Drawing on scholars from diverse disciplines, we conducted a series of case studies and corporate interviews in the United States, Europe, Australia, and Asia to determine the extent of corporate response to terrorism. Our goal was to begin to understand corporate priorities (such as survival, resilience, rebuilding) and to identify best practices in the management of corporate exposure to terrorism. Initially, and consistent with other research, we discovered that few firms are taking steps to deal specifically with terrorism. For example, in interviews with the largest firms in their respective industries in France, we learned that top managers have no specific plans to safeguard against terrorism.

Our research at various multinational firms uncovered foreign subsidiary managers who shunt any terrorism concerns off onto headquarters. We encountered top level global managers who frame terrorism only in direct, local terms and look for local managers to address possible repercussions. We encountered circumstances where substantial initiatives had been undertaken to develop greater security and scrutiny on a corporate level, yet international management did little to help defray the growing expenses of this increased sensitivity. In one instance, the increased cost led only to the wholesale closure of international operations due to the lack of return on investment. In Europe and Japan, we even encountered firms that saw terrorism as strictly an American problem.

However, our findings reveal that terrorism is a real, global concern, and firms that believe themselves immune are likely to encounter difficulties in the longer term. The goals of terrorists are too broad and too sinister to permit managerial indifference. Terrorists strike at innocent victims in order to sow fear and uncertainty. An unprepared target is more attractive to a terrorist. The lethality and scale of the type of weapons available and the callousness in using them herald a new era.

Increasing Terrorism

Modern terrorists attack businesses more than any other type of target. In fact, there were more than 300 attacks against businesses each year during the last decade. Latin America experiences most events, followed by Western Europe, Asia, and the Middle East. According to Patterns of Global Terrorism, a yearly report issued by the U.S. State Department, bombings are most common, followed by armed attacks, kidnapping, vandalism, and hijacking.

Realistically, however, the risk of direct harm to individual firms from terrorism remains relatively small. The main impact will likely come from the indirect effects of terrorism. Indirect effects include sharp reductions in buyer demand for both consumer and industrial goods that result from the fear and panic caused by terrorist acts. Many activities slow down or come to a halt--we call that the "chill effect."

There are many indirect effects of terrorism that affect marketing, including:

Unpredictable shifts or interruptions in the supply of needed inputs, resources, and services. For multinational firms, interruptions may result from delays in customs clearance as increased security measures lessen the efficiency of supply chains and logistics. For example, the severe tightening of border controls following the 9/11 attacks, especially at the United States/Canada border, resulted in long waiting times that disrupted operations in numerous manufacturing firms.

Failures in power, communications, transportation, and other infrastructures. For example, lower Manhattan relied almost entirely on Verizon in telecommunications and Con Edison in electricity, both of which sustained substantial damage in the 9/11 attacks, cutting services for long periods. A January 2002 report from Global Insight Inc. (formerly Data Resources Inc. and Wharton Econometric Forecasting Associates) for the New York State Senate Finance Committee, "Financial Impact of World Trade Center Attack," states that it took years to return these systems to pre-9/11 levels.

Government policies and laws enacted to deal with terrorism. These can alter the business environment and the ease with which marketing, especially international marketing, is conducted. New regulations and policies increase costs and affect the commercial environment in ways that may be more harmful to business than the terrorist events that provoked them. For example, the security measures of the U.S. government's air cargo security plan have substantially increased transportation and logistics costs and may increase the cost of trading internationally by as much as 3%.

Macroeconomic phenomena. This can include such (real or per-ceived) phenomena as declining per-capita income, decreased purchasing power, or falling stock market values. Such trends directly create buyer uncertainty about the state of national economies.

Deteriorating relations among countries. This affects foreign buyer attitudes and the marketing activities of firms doing business abroad. For example, the 9/11 attacks and subsequent events changed relations be-tween the United States and several Middle Eastern countries, further affecting the effectiveness and efficiency of value-chain and marketing activities.

Marketing Implications

Terrorism will increasingly influence the evaluation and selection of mar-kets, particularly those located abroad. Developing nations tend to be most vulnerable to economic and consumption downturns following terrorist events. Businesses will be affected by new, government-imposed regulations and policies that produce increased transactional friction in value chain activities. As regulators have only limited experience with ter-rorism, the new rules are likely to cause much collateral damage--at least initially.

Buyers affected by terrorism may be unable to fulfill contracts or pur-chase new merchandise. There will be a tendency, therefore, for firms to develop trade portfolios for both the supply and demand sides of their operations. The twin goals of these portfolios will be to limit dependence on regions or customers that might be susceptible to interruptions and to systematically develop markets as a means of diversifying risk by balanc-ing existing exposures.

Terrorism, even at distant locations, can induce shortages or delays of input goods that disrupt critical company operations. Distribution and lo-gistics are particularly vulnerable because governments impose regulations and restrictions that affect the timing and efficiency of such activities, par-ticularly from international sources. Following 9/11, for example, tighter security at U.S. customs checkpoints prompted long shipping delays, which forced Ford Motor Co. to temporarily close five of its U.S. auto plants.

Risk is difficult to assess in an integrated global economy where supply chains are complex and producers rely on suppliers and supplier's suppliers at locations across the globe. The more a firm relies on international sources of supply, the greater the vulnerability of inventory stocks. The more that suppliers are seen as vulnerable, the less likely buyers will be to purchase goods from those suppliers.

Coping Proactively

In the wake of a typical terrorist event, buildings must be rebuilt, security arrangements must be enhanced, and risk premiums must be assessed. Although always regrettable, terrorism nevertheless creates new opportunities for firms in a few industries, such as construction, security, and information technology. For most companies, however, terrorism results in reduced revenues or increased costs, and it's these consequences for which managers must prepare. Firms should prepare to deal with the "before and after" of terrorism via appropriate marketing strategies and practices.

Before Attack

Managers must consider the possibility of terrorism in overall strategic and portfolio planning. Scenario planning can be instrumental in encouraging preparedness and rapid response to changing conditions. Strategy and practice are best determined through market research and assessment of the basic nature of each location, industry characteristics, and the level of risk that management is willing to tolerate. This includes scanning to anticipate the likely consequences--primarily indirect effects--of future terrorist events. Regularly scanning and forecasting emerging business conditions is critical, especially for firms that rely heavily on foreign-sourced raw materials and other input goods. Preparing for terrorism involves expenditures that may prove unnecessary in the long run. Cost-benefit analysis, therefore, is useful for determining the optimal balance between the cost of preparing for terrorism and the consequences of terrorism.

To scan for terrorism-related threats, access various resources online and elsewhere. For instance, the U.S. State Department (www.state.gov)

provides information and links on background and requirements for international travel and business, especially concerning conditions abroad that may affect safety and security. The U.S. Department of Homeland Security (www.dhs.gov) provides similar but more specific information about potential and actual threats of terrorism in nations around the world. The Center for Strategic and International Studies (www.csis.org) offers strategic insights and possible solutions for current and emerging global threats. CSIS also provides resources and analyses on terrorism-related threats, such as its recent publication, Data Mining and Data Analysis for Counterterrorism . GlobalEdge at Michigan State University (globaledge.msu.edu) provides links to hundreds of sites and documents that can assist in analysis.

The threat level of terrorism should be used as a segmentation variable when evaluating new markets, particularly those located in risky areas. Highly vulnerable markets should be avoided or assigned risk premiums. Terrorism should be considered when designing and developing supply chains and distribution channels. Risk premiums should be considered when developing foreign-based production or marketing facilities at relatively hazardous locations. Terrorism should influence planning the location of foreign subsidiaries, proposed target markets, and especially international distribution channels and supply-chain management. For example, following recent terrorist events, toy manufacturing giant Hasbro invested considerable sums in planning and implementation to ensure the integrity of its extensive global supply chain.

Flexibility is critical in supply-chain management for dealing with terrorism. This requires the ability to address the demands of specific situations by redefining positioning and refocusing resources in the midst of dynamic circumstances, shocks, and traumas. Flexibility means having the ability to source from various suppliers and/or shift production to different regions in the wake of unanticipated disruptive events. Skillful supply-chain management is critical to ensuring no interruptions occur and normal customer service levels are maintained in the wake of terrorism's direct and indirect effects. For example, Compaq (now part of Hewlett-Packard) established secondary suppliers for all of its critical computer input components. The firm also owns assembly operations in various locations worldwide. Management can quickly shift production

from one locale to another in the event of a crisis. Such flexibility mini-
mizes the possibility that Compaq's operations will be interrupted in the
event of a terrorist attack.

The threat of terrorism means that firms should source from a wider
range of suppliers located in a wider range of locations, or from more
familiar, "safer" sources of supply. Purchasing managers should maintain
larger safety stocks of essential inputs or develop multiple supply sources
for vulnerable input goods as a cushion against terrorism's effects. Manufacturers should regularly reevaluate transportation and shipping arrangements. Logisticians should emphasize total supply network visibility so
they can quickly identify and respond to actual or potential problems. In
the long run, manufacturers may even consider producing more essential
inputs themselves, as opposed to buying them from suppliers.

Flexibility here also means the ability to shift to different transportation modes to deal with terrorism-related interruptions. For instance,
Chrysler used expedited truck service to move parts normally shipped
by air following the 9/11 attack. Contractual arrangements for volume
increases or expedited service from suppliers are also useful. One firm has
contractual arrangements with all its suppliers to provide supply capacity
increases up to 25% in one week's time, and 100% in four weeks. The
Center for Transportation and Logistics at the Massachusetts Institute of
Technology reports another firm contracted to have dedicated 747 airlin-
ers (available within 48 hours), in case of delay or unavailability of regular
supply channels.

Logistics software is extremely helpful for global tracking and for providing guidance when disruptions occur. Radio frequency identification
(RFID) technology allows manufacturers to track shipments, monitor and
detect specific supply-chain events, manage order and delivery processes,
and help with fulfillment, transportation, and pricing optimization. Par-
tially in response to the threat of terrorism, Wal-Mart now requires all of
its suppliers to tag all shipping cases and palettes with RFID. Purchasing
managers can also emphasize operational methods less sensitive to terrorism, such as video-conferencing, e-mailing, and online trading.

Increased collaboration with local partners can help mitigate the harm
of terrorism. For example, Hewlett-Packard now relies on linkages with
backup U.S.-based suppliers of inkjet printers in addition to a Singapore

firm that handles most of the firm's stable production. Risk sharing is possible in instances of major terrorist interruption of corporate activities. In particular, firms with long-standing customer-supplier relationships should cooperate to reduce exposure to interruptions in normal value-chain activities. Formal preparatory exercises can help reduce the number of surprises in real circumstances.

Firms must focus more on innovative collaboration schemes and other inter-organizational support systems. Increasing interaction between enterprises in the supply chain improves coordination and reduces the threat of shocks and interruptions. Co-managed inventory in the retail sector, just-in-time manufacturing, and collaborative transportation management in the transportation industry are a few examples. Such initiatives aim to ensure that trading partners share information and coordinate forecasts to avoid unnecessary inventory fluctuations. For example, following 9/11, Toyota Motor Corp. worked with its top suppliers to develop security plans that offer alternative arrangements in the event of supply interruptions. This represents a major shift in company strategy from just-in-time to "just-in-case" planning.

The Internet and other forms of information technology are especially instrumental in facilitating increased collaboration. In the wake of terrorist events and to the extent lead times become more variable and forecasts less certain, companies should redouble their collaborative efforts. Moreover, collaboration among industry groups and public policy makers will facilitate the development of best security practices and shared expertise. Industry needs to be aware of policy concerns, just as policy makers need to appreciate industry sensitivities. Without ongoing direct communication, each group is likely to make major culture-bound mistakes.

Terrorists increasingly use the Internet and e-mail for perpetrating their ends. Companies in the services sector that rely heavily on information technology and linkages over the Internet must guard against acts of cyber-terrorism, such as launching viruses via the World Wide Web. Following 9/11, the Ohio Savings Bank ($13.3 billion in assets) implemented contingency planning and disaster recovery solutions. The bank now stores critical data in several locations that can be immediately accessed in the event of disaster. Similarly, Georgetown University in Washington, D.C., has prepared for terrorist interruptions through intense faculty training and the wide distribution of computer servers to ensure continuity of operations. It's worth the up-front investment to establish Web sites, interactive product catalogues, and other cyber-offerings that are secure and impervious to harmful activities of hackers and terrorists. Some firms actively test their information technology systems by using third party audits, emergency shutdown drills, and third party hackers to assess their vulnerability to break-in and access.

After Attack

Buyers tend to reduce consumption after a large-scale terrorist event. Marketing communications and public relations are extremely important recovery activities. Management should put in place contingency plans to deal with buyer panic and uncertainty. Short-term promotional activities may play an important role in encouraging reluctant consumers to resume normal buying. Appropriately crafted marketing communications contribute significantly toward reducing buyer dissonance and hesitation. Post-terrorism marketing activities should be initiated early to calm customers, as well as encourage their continued patronage.

Following 9/11, for example, monthly revenue in the Washington, D.C., hotel industry dropped dramatically but recovered within a few months thanks to a coordinated effort of local hotels, tourism agencies, and the government to promote tourism in the D.C. area. According to a 2002 article in the Cornell Hotel and Restaurant Administrative Quarterly , marketing activities included (1) a coordinated response among key industry players, (2) lobbying and campaigning to reopen and reinvigorate major tourist attractions, (3) promoting travel to the region through innovative marketing campaigns, and (4) developing broader marketing plans and strategies to promote the area as a "must-visit destination."

The 9/11 attacks revealed the importance of providing extraordinary customer service, especially if the nature of the business is critical to reestablishing public confidence after a catastrophe occurs. Within hours of the 9/11 attack, Dell, Hewlett-Packard, and IBM set up emergency response centers and hired call handlers to deal with the tremendous influx of emergency inquiries from worried customers.

Following the 9/11 attacks, the Internet proved to be more reliable than telephone lines and other instant communication means.

It's extremely useful, therefore, for facilitating marketing communications in the period immediately following terrorist attacks. For instance, General Motors and General Electric employed their Web sites extensively following 9/11 to communicate with key customers and supply-chain members.

Marketers may pursue a strategy of retargeting offerings to segments less sensitive to terrorism. In the months following 9/11, for example, marketers in the hotel industry focused selling efforts on getting regional rather than international or national business to shore up lost sales. In other industries, marketers can refocus sales efforts on safer domestic markets--markets that are well-known or closer to home.

In some industries, managers use price discounting to attract buyers who reduce consumption during difficult periods. For example, firms in the tourism sector reduced prices to encourage renewed consumption following the 9/11 attacks. Lower prices can be achieved via cost cutting. For example, in the hotel industry, managers cut costs by reducing workers' hours. In the wake of the 9/11 attacks, the OECD (Organisation for Economic Co-operation and Development) reported that the airline industry substantially curtailed capacity, with available seat miles falling by about 15% in the ensuing months. Additional cost-reducing measures might include putting off unneeded or expensive projects. These efforts help to reduce pressures to increase pricing after terrorist events.

Unfortunately for most industries, however, increased restrictions in customs clearance, costs related to increased security measures, higher pricing for certain input goods (due to various terrorism-related factors), and activities associated with recovery marketing, all exert upward pressure on the pricing of goods to end users. Because managers are averse to risk, they will tend to charge higher prices for goods that appear susceptible to higher levels of terrorism exposure. For example, financial services, insurance, real estate, travel packages, international transportation, and similar services are vulnerable to the extent they are offered in high-risk areas or are tied to specific risk-prone locations. Certain commodities (such as oil, base minerals, agricultural goods) may be subject to shortages and incur higher prices in the wake of terrorism. Ultimately, terrorism will lead to price tension effects as increased costs, lower utilization, and other factors encourage higher prices, while efforts to mitigate falling demand will encourage price discounting.

Going Forward

Terrorism increases transactions costs and creates trade barriers. Despite its potential impact, however, there is limited research on the link between terrorism and marketing. We need more insights on the level of the firm--we need to better understand how companies and managers can prepare themselves for the unthinkable.

Research is needed now more than ever on how to best optimize managerial practice in light of terrorist threats. As responsible marketing managers, we cannot stand by and say, "It's unlikely to happen to my company, and there's nothing cost-effective I can do anyway." Marketers must reach across organizations, not just to their marketing partners but also to others in their industry or locality. There should be a sharing of both development expense and expertise.

Terrorism and its effects are much too important to be left to corporate strategists. It's marketers who are confronted with terrorism on a daily basis in terms of demand and supply. Marketers are the ones to respond to threats by devising new distribution and logistics avenues. Communicating with buyers and suppliers and responding with pricing strategies to market dislocation are both marketing activities.

Marketers also bring to the table their understanding of empathy and culture. For example, in an analysis of the strength and resilience of a supply chain, it's marketers who will not only check how important a given supplier is to the firm but also ask how important the firm and its account are to the supplier. Marketers also can find approaches to change the value of the relationship. And it's marketers who understand the difference in objectives by various segments and populations, be they domestic or international. It is, for example, our task to work with physicians to develop their activities for a vaccination program in case of a national emergency. But it takes a marketer to appreciate the logistical issue of ensuring that the vaccine is widely available. We have the capability and talent to help combat terrorism. As a passenger on the hijacked flight over Pennsylvania said on 9/11 before fighting back the terrorists, "Let's roll!"

Armenian News, August 28, 2014

by Armenian News

The conflicts between Russia and Ukraine, has led to Western against Russia. Some Russian officials no longer can travel abroad, and international investment and trade are restricted. Russian President Vladimir Putin, in turn, plans retaliatory sanctions against the U.S. and Western Europe by restricting Russian food imports and energy exports.

Governments attempt to impose comparable sanction burdens on each other. However, due to cultural and historic differences, a policy based mainly on sanctions will lead to inequities and substantially therefore increase the risk in international trade.

Key differences exist between Russia and western nations regarding profit, competition, risk and reward, private property and growth, and how they affect the outcome of sanctions.

In the U.S., profit is the expected result of doing business, and low profits are usually blamed on management. By contrast, lower profits in Russia allows its government to shift the blame onto foreign culprits.

Private property is a key reward in the United States, while in Russia 'private' often means responsibility and risk exposure. Since growth is key in the U.S., any inhibitors of growth are seen with concern. A wide variety of economic performance in Russia, makes its growth much less of a pressure point.

Sanctions against the U.S. may burden the population and lead to new candidates and policies. In Russia, the sacrifices imposed by sanctions seem to indicate dedication and strength. Declining U.S. profits or growth cause doomsday scenarios, while time is expected to bring economic improvement.

Losing out on the very latest technology means falling behind for Americans. For Russians, pretty good technology is a pretty good achievement. Russian ownership of space ferries and satellites and their use by the U.S. makes them proud.

Russia's size of 6.6 million square miles makes it the largest country in the world. The 300 million U.S. population more than doubles that of Russia. Still, the Russian market is of great importance for many global firms.

There are only few historical rewards for former leaders. For example, though Greece invented the Olympic Games, no points are given for that ancient super action. Going first with the Greek flag when marching into the Olympic Stadium is just about all there is. Russia may well see its existing strength and market size as an opportunity for leadership.

We all are said to understand each other so much better than in the past. Yet, much of our thinking is based on our history, culture and outlook. They define our spheres of interest which we aim to preserve. Ukraine, for example, will tend to be closer to Russia than to the United States. The average Russian understands as much about Columbus, Ohio as the average American does about Sevastopol.

Global relationships between Russia, Asia, Europe and the United States are being re-balanced. Key changes are likely to come from outside the United States. It would be unwise to undertake transformations without dampening the key concerns of key players on all sides.

Success in the Battle Against Counterfeits
(With Alexandria Times October 31, 2014)

The problem of fake or counterfeit products and services is an international plague. Companies keep facing counterfeit product issues with the aim of verifying sellers and protecting buyers. It is no longer just the United States and companies in highly post-industrialized countries where the problem of misleading merchandise stands in the foreground. China's biggest Internet companies have clamped down on a problem that has hit China's e-commerce market particularly hard. Common scams involve posting fake ads to draw unsuspecting consumers, selling knockoffs or accepting payments for products that are never delivered. Alibaba, China's largest Internet trading firm is striving to project a clean image and increase oversight as this e-commerce platform moves toward the world's largest public offerings ever. Alibaba spends more than $16 million yearly fighting counterfeit goods; particularly on Taobao, its biggest shopping site.

With the globalization of competition, new markets, especially in emerging countries, have become both recipients and originators of products with intellectual property. Just consider the value of African music components that have been integrated into Western melodies. The communication revolution, emanating from the growth of digital and on-line technologies, has made of intellectual property both easier to distribute and more difficult to control.

One can also observe that many countries, particularly poorer ones, are reluctant, and often unable to pay for intellectual property. As these countries grow and develop their indigenous innovations, they also grow in their understanding of the IP issue, their need to protect their own IP, and develop a willingness to pay for IP. We are seeing a gradual shift from the unwilling to the willing, so the future looks bright.

Strategic and Effective Responses

It takes effective intellectual property enforcement to ensure that a revolutionary idea can blossom into economic opportunity and to allow the innovative spirit to create the good, high-paying jobs that will drive our prosperity in this Century. Effective enforcement in turn requires understanding the nature of the threat. Intellectual Property Rights (IPRs) have become a core issue in the economic debate: the front pages of newspapers continually report major controversies among corporations, governments and consumers. No longer confined to cheap knockoffs of luxury goods, IP theft is putting industry and the public at risk of highly adverse economic, safety, and health consequences.

Counterfeit goods are any goods bearing an unauthorized representation of a trademark, patented invention, or copyrighted work that is legally protected in the country where it is marketed. Globally, companies reportedly lose a total of $657 billion every year because of product counterfeiting and other infringement on intellectual property. IPR violations have spread to high-technology products and services from the traditionally counterfeited products. Today's key problems are with high-visibility and strong brand name consumer goods. In addition, previously the only concern was whether a company's product was being counterfeited; now, companies have to worry about whether the raw materials and components purchased for production are themselves genuine. The European Union estimates that trade in counterfeit goods now accounts for 2 percent of total world trade. The International Chamber of Commerce estimates the figure at 5–7 percent. In general, countries with lower per capita incomes, higher levels of corruption in government, and lower levels of involvement in international trade tend to have more intellectual property violations.

After securing valuable intellectual property rights, the international marketer must act to enforce these rights. Types of action against counterfeiting are legal remedies, bilateral and multilateral negotiations, joint private sector action, and administrative measures encouraged by individual companies. It is essential that all the parties interact to gain the most effect. A multi-dimensional threat requires a multi-dimensional response. No industry or country is immune from the threat, nor can they address the threat alone. One needs increased cooperation of affected parties, as well as increased resources and improved tools to tackle the growing and evolving nature of the threat. There is also need for better education regarding the risks IPR violations pose and how to defend against them. The following analysis provides a detailed basis for developing more strategic and effective responses to the burgeoning threat.

Legislative and Enforcement

For example, the pharmaceutical industry lobbied to make sure that provisions for patent protection in the NAFTA agreement were meticulously spelled out.

PhRMA (Pharmaceutical Research and Manufacturers) addressed the issue of international IP protection by responding to the Special 301 Report issued by the United States Trade Representative (USTR) in May 2012. PhRMA noted that: "The Special 301 process continues to be effective in gaining high-level attention from our trading partners—attention that is needed to redress intellectual property violations and market access concerns." The PhRMA statement cited the need for IP protections in spurring innovation, research and development, as well as the need for fair international market conditions to ensure that patients have access to medications.

The World Health Organization defines counterfeit pharmaceuticals as medicines that have been deliberately and fraudulently mislabeled as to identity or source in an effort to make them appear to be genuine. The Food and Drug Administration defines counterfeit pharmaceuticals as drugs that are produced, distributed, or sold under a product name without authorization from the rights holder and where the identity of the drug source is knowingly and intentionally mislabeled in a way that suggests it is the authentic and approved product. One research firm estimated the global market for counterfeit pharmaceuticals to generate revenues between $75 billion and $200 billion a year. The Pharmaceutical Security Institute (PSI), a pharmaceutical trade association created to address illegal pharmaceutical incidents, collects data on the number of counterfeiting, illegal diversion, and theft incidents. These incidents increased seventy-eight percent from 2005 to 2009. Pfizer reports that between 2004 and 2010 it seized more than 62 million doses of counterfeit medicines worldwide. More than 200 million counterfeit Eli Lilly medicines have been seized in 800 raids around the world.

Illegal Internet pharmacies conceal their real identity, are operated internationally, sell medications without prescriptions, and deliver products with unknown and unpredictable origins or history. These sites are particularly dangerous because consumers generally have no way to determine what is in the medicines they receive. Consumers do not understand the risk of purchasing drugs from these sites. Sixty-three percent of Americans surveyed reported hearing nothing or very little about prescription drugs being made with ingredients that make them unsafe to consume. Also in case of problems, where can the suffering consumer seek recourse?

Educate

Asia's World City, Hong Kong is committed to the protection of intellectual property. With the goal of enhancing consumer confidence in Hong Kong, and to strengthen the City's reputation as a "Shopping Paradise" for genuine products, the Intellectual Property Department has launched the "No Fakes Pledge" Scheme.

The scheme was established in 1998. The issuing bodies of the "No Fakes Pledge" Scheme are the *Hong Kong & Kowloon Electrical Appliances Merchants' Association Limited* and the *Hong Kong Coalition for Intellectual Property Rights of the Federation of Hong Kong Industries*. The "No Fakes Pledge" Scheme not only aims to promote a sense of pride among traders who do not deal in counterfeit and pirated goods; it also aims to enhance awareness of intellectual property protection among retailers and consumers alike.

The "No Fakes Pledge" scheme campaign encourages participating retail merchants to set a good example by pledging not to sell or distribute counterfeit or pirated products, thus establishing and upholding honest and trustworthy trading practices. With the help of strong marketing and growing participation, this campaign further distinguishes honest and reliable retail merchants, thereby gaining the confidence and trust of consumers.

In 2004, the Hong Kong Intellectual Property Department cooperated with the Guangdong Intellectual Property Office to launch the "No Fakes Pledge" Scheme in Guangdong Province. In 2011, the Guangdong Intellectual Property Office (GIPO), Copyright Bureau of Guangdong Province (GDCB) and Guangdong Province Administration for Industry and Commerce (GDAIC) jointly announced the launch of the "No Fakes Pledge" Scheme in all 21 cities at the prefectural level in Guangdong Province, as well as Shunde District, Foshan.

All participating retail merchants of the "No Fakes Pledge" Scheme have committed not to sell or deal in counterfeit or pirated goods and to sell only genuine goods. All retail merchants participating in the "No Fakes Pledge" Scheme will post the "No Fakes" stickers and tent cards in their shops. With the "No Fakes" logo, tourists and consumers can easily identify reliable retailers and shop with confidence.

Public and Private Sector Interaction

A number of other governments are drafting similar policies, which have served as a catalyst for enhancing protection in both the public and private sectors in those nations. Efforts to protect intellectual property, and modernize the patent and trademark system are crucial. The power of creativity and innovation applied to the expression or the solving of practical problems is not the exclusive province of any country or people, but is a resource of limitless potential available to everyone. A victory over fakes and counterfeits will protect the quality and reliability of products and services, and lets customers be more informed and secure in their usage decisions.

SECTION 5

On Freedom and Economic Growth

On Freedom and International Marketing

Originally Published by the Congressional Record

You may ask what freedom has to do with international marketing. Freedom is about options. If there is no alternative, there is no freedom. A true alternative provides the opportunity to make a decision, to exercise virtue. In the blaze of the klieg lights, it is easy to make the "right" decision. That's not an exercise in virtue, because real alternatives are effectively removed. The true selection among alternatives takes place in the darkness of night when nobody is looking.

The focus and aim of international marketing is on crossing borders. The goal is to provide more than one choice for customers, letting them pick from a selection of options in order to maximize their satisfaction. International marketing does so in all comers of the globe, the glamorous ones as well as in the small and remote ones where the efforts are not seen by others. By operating both in the limelight and also well outside of it, international marketing offers the freedom to exercise virtue both to the seller and the buyer--be it in decisions of supplying or purchasing, pricing or selecting.

Another key dimension of freedom is not to confine, allowing people to go outside of the box. As a concept, freedom knows no international boundaries. But national borders usually are the box where business and government find their limits. Such borders are a mere point of transition for international marketing. The discipline thrives on understanding of how to successfully cross national borders, on coping with the differences once the crossing is done, and on profitably reconciling any conflicts.

International marketing contains the freedom of almost unlimited growth potential. Activities confined to domestic borders may well run into limits of expansion. International market opportunities relax these limits quickly. Instead of restrictions, the international marketing paradigm encourages the stripping away of restraints; instead of limitations, there is the encounter of opportunity.

Freedom also means not being forced to do something one does not want to do (Hayek, 1971). There are economic migration pressures that force people to move from their rural homes into urban areas or from their developing countries into industrialized ones. Industrialized nations, in turn, speak about immigration pressure. For both sides, little if any freedom is involved here. Most individuals who do the moving would much rather stay home but cannot afford to do so due to economic exigencies. The recipient countries might not want to welcome the migrants but do so in response to political and humanitarian pressures. International marketing may have been part of what triggered some of these migrations, but it also can be instrumental in stemming the tide. It can provide the economic opportunity for individuals at home so that they need not migrate. Thus, it lets individuals become productive contributors to the global economy free from pressures to shift locations.

When the long-standing rivalry between socialism and market orientation was resolved, market forces and the recognition of demand and supply directly affected human rights and the extent of freedom. With all humility and gratefulness we can conclude: Markets were right! In country after country, market forces have demonstrated typically greater efficiency and effectiveness in their ability to satisfy the needs of people.

International marketing has been instrumental in stimulating these newly emerging market forces. In spite of complaints about the slowness of change, the insufficiency of wealth redistribution, and the inequities inherent in societal upheavals, a large majority of participants in market-oriented changes are now better off than they were before. Without the transition provided by international marketing, these changes would not have come about that swiftly.

The Cost of Freedom

One keeps healing about the large segment of the world population that is poor and therefore supposedly excluded from any international marketing efforts; the World Bank's former president called them the 3 billion $2-a-day poor (Wolfensohn, 2001). By contrast, international marketers see them as an attractive $6 billion-a-day opportunity for valuable exchanges!

What's more is that international marketing provides the opportunity to acquire resources without the deployment of force. Why fight if you can trade? Countries that have been historic enemies such as France, England and Germany are now all united in their close collaboration through international marketing. (Farmer, 1987) The field is, therefore, at the very least contributing to freedom from war while providing additional choices for consumption.

But the cost of freedom is rising. Terms like free trade or free choice are misleading since they all come with a price, which international marketers pay in terms of preparing their shipments, scrutinizing their customers, and conforming to government regulations.

We all are paying a higher price due to global terrorism. As freedom suffers, so does international marketing. In most instances, terrorism is not an outgrowth of choice but rather the lack of it. Terrorists may succeed in reducing the freedom of others but not in increasing their own. Who is typically most affected by terrorist acts? Attacks aimed at businesses, such as the infamous bombings of U.S. franchises abroad, do not bring big corporations to their knees. The local participants, the local employees, the local investors, and the local customers are affected most. Who can protect themselves against such attacks and who can afford to protect targets? Only the more wealthy countries and companies can. They have the choice of where to place their funds, with whom to trade, and whether to hold the enemy at bay through a security bubble created by changing business forn1ats via exporting or franchising. The poor players do not have choices. The local firms, the nations with economies in development, and the poor customers continue to be exposed to further acts of terrorism with very limited indigenous ability to influence events.

But international marketing can enable the disenfranchised to develop alternatives. Multinational firms can invest in the world's poorest markets and increase their own revenue while reducing poverty. With support from shareholders and the benefit of good governance, international marketers can, and should, continue in their role as social change agents. The discipline has value maximization at its heart. If it is worthwhile to fulfill the needs of large segments of people, even at low margins, then it will be done. International marketers after all have as their key desire the creation of new customers and suppliers and they are delighted when, in fulfillment of their aims, they can bring about freedom from extremes of hunger, sickness, and intolerance. Value and Freedom

In a global setting, freedom can take on many dimensions. Privileges and obligations that are near and dear to some may well be cheap and easily disposed of by others. The views of one society may differ from views held in other regions of the world. Such differences then account for misunderstandings, surprises, and long-term conflicts.

There are two value dimensions at work here, both of them highly relevant to international marketing. One may be circumscribed as the freedom and values of a market economy. To make them work governmental, managerial, and corporate virtue, vision, and veracity are required. Unless the world can believe in what institutions and their leaders say and do, it will be difficult to forge a global commitment between those doing the marketing and the ones being marketed to. It is therefore of vital interest to the proponents of freedom and international marketing to ensure that corruption, bribery, lack of transparency, and poor governance are exposed for their negative effects in any setting or society. The main remedy will be the collaboration of the global policy community in agreeing on what constitutes transgressions and swift punishment of the culprits involved, so that market forces can work free from distortion.

A second and even more crucial issue is the value system we use in making choices. Some years ago, the Mars Climate Orbiter mission failed spectacularly as a result of the use of different values by the mission navigation teams. One team was using metric units and the other used the English system of measurement. This mistake caused the orbiter to get too close to the atmosphere, where it was destroyed ("NASA's Metric Confusion," 1999).

There are major differences among what people value around the world. Contrasts include togetherness next to individuality, cooperation next to competition, modesty next to assertiveness, and self-effacement next to self-actualization. Often, global differences in value systems keep us apart and result in spectacularly destructive differences. How we value a life, for example, can be crucial in terms of how we treat individuals. What value we place on family, work, leisure time, or progress has a substantial effect on how we see and evaluate each other.

Cultural studies tell us that there are major differences between and even within nations. International marketing, through its linkages via goods, services, ideas, and communications, can achieve important assimilations of value systems. On the consumer side, new products offer international appeal and encourage similar activities around the world: many of us wear denim, dance the same dances, and eat pizza and sushi (Marquardt & Reynolds, 1994). It has been claimed that local product offerings help define people and provide identity and that it is the local idiosyncrasies that make people beautiful (Johansson, 2004). Some even offer the persistence of the specific breakfast habits of the English and the French as evidence of local immutability in the face of globalization (de Mooij, 1998). Yet, we should remember that values are learned, not genetically implanted. As life's experiences grow more international and more similar, so do values. Therefore, every time international marketing forges a new linkage in thinking, new progress is made in shaping a greater global commonality in values. It may well be that international marketing's ability to align global values which makes it easier for countries, companies, and individuals to build bridges between them, may eventually become the field's greatest gift to the world. A joined occurrence

How do freedom and international marketing match with today's discontent so forcefully expressed by the disgruntlement of the anti-globalists? Many claim that never before in history has there been so much evidence about such strong opposition to globalization and to Americans as harbingers of international marketing.

Perhaps those making such claims are sadly mistaken. In looking at other "globalizers" in world history, such as the Vikings, the Mongols, the Tatars, and the Romans, there probably was both intellectual and physical opposition (or do we really believe that everybody enjoyed Genghis Khan?). But protest was never allowed to become very vocal, or to engage in repeated, large demonstrations or widespread pamphleteering. Due to rather harsh policies of dealing with the opposition, very few records of such resistance are available today. Consequently, comparisons with past events are difficult to make and are likely to be highly inaccurate.

Today's news is good. The nations, institutions and individuals around the world are increasingly accepting freedom as the key foundation of the good life. We are discovering that international marketing, both as a discipline and as an activity is very closely interwoven with freedom—some even call it essential. It is the freedom Thomas Aquinas saw as the means to human excellence and happiness (Weigel, 2001) which international marketing helps us reach. In reciprocal causality, freedom causes and facilitates international marketing, while international marketing is a key support of the cause of freedom. A productive symbiosis at work!

How Economic Growth Becomes Visible

(With Roger Blackwell)
Originally Published in Korea Times

Media tend to attribute economic health to political leaders, parliament or central banks, but marketers know that consumers control 70 percent or more of GDP in mature economies. Traditional economic analyses focus on fiscal and monetary policies. Marketers and behavioral economists believe that consumers and their migration dominate global markets now and in the future.

The European industrial revolution two centuries ago transformed agricultural workers, who produced most of their own consumption needs, to city-dwellers who bought products and created markets. The rural-urban migration surfaced in North America the past century, fueled by the automobile. In Japan, the ultimate victors were Seibu and Takashimaya; in Europe, they were Ikea and Carrefour. In the U.S., it was Walmart and specialty chains as varied as Home Depot and Victoria's

Secret. Firms from three continents compete today for similar segments around the world, serving consumers converted from self-produced goods and services, (both unseen and non-monetized), to marketer-produced products. Just because home-produced products are "unseen" in a nation's GDP does not mean they do not exist.

Production and consumption once monetized and measured become visible because they now are recognized in the GDP. Such a shift leads to a more systematic sector approach by producers, greater selectivity by consumers and more specific attention and measures taken by policymakers, all of which leads to substantial GDP growth.

During such a growth process, exports often "prime the pump" and become a magnet for urban migration. But blazing GDP growth is powered by domestic sales to domestic consumers. Marketers propose, but consumers dispose, and determine the growth of economies and health of individual firms.

U.S. GDP grew rapidly in past decades mostly because the proportion of urban baby-boomer women working outside their homes went from minuscule to massive. Food preparation, child-care, home maintenance and transportation changed from non-monetized to measured labor. GDP soared with mountains of markets for goods and services ranging from autos, refrigerators and automatic washing machines to restaurants, prepared foods and grocery stores, along with health care, lawn services, child-care and cleaning, mostly bought by consumers formerly producing those products themselves.

Around the turn of the current century, China activated a similar conversion from self-production to industrial production for 125 million consumers moving to cities, estimated by China experts to reach 700 million by 2020. With relaxed consent for Foreign Direct Investment (FDI) and a projected population in India of two billion by 2050, the axis of GDP growth moves east fast.

Urban migration is igniting emerging markets ranging from Vietnam and Ghana and other African nations to countries in Latin America and the Middle East. Monetary and fiscal policies provide the rails for GDP growth, but the locomotive is urban consumers. When hyper-stimulation of easy credit and excessive debt stokes the engine too fast, the economy risks a train wreck, as the United States, Greece, Spain and other nations have discovered. When economists do not understand the behavior and temporal role of consumers, they risk prescribing the wrong cure for the new norm in mature economies of slow-growth GDP and fewer jobs.

The transition from self-producing agrarian economies to urban societies with marketer-produced products greatly affects GDP and jobs. Most markets in Europe and North America have reached the upper limits in rural-urban migration, suggesting the same conclusion about GDP growth. Naive critics complain, "We don't make anything in this country anymore" hoping to return factory jobs to past levels. In fact, U.S. factories are producing more than any time in history. Output doubled the past three decades, but factory employees declined by a third. The way for mature economies to compete with emerging countries is to reduce labor content, continuing exactly what the U.S. has already done in both agriculture and manufacturing.

A century ago, 70 percent of the labor force worked on the farm. Today, 1.8 percent of the labor force produces so much output that the nation's greatest health problem is obesity, with ample surplus to export. Manufacturing employed 30 percent of the nation's workers in 1950, dropping to 9 percent by 2010, headed to the same level as agriculture. Banks are rising in terms of revenues and profits, but project substantial job reductions of 25 percent in five years. Productivity produces higher paying jobs, but there are fewer of them. Booms of a prosperous middle class are identifiable in India, Bangladesh, Mexico, Turkey, Colombia, Thailand, Ghana, Nigeria and other nations.

International marketers should identify both the industry and location where there is a transition of human activity from invisible and unmeasured to visible and the transition is measured and recognized. We must also understand the temporal nature of societal shifts and migration, a reversal or limitation of which is likely to ring in major changes as well.

Of Chicken Slaughter and NSA Wiretaps: Do We Really Want to Know?

Originally Published in Ovi Magazine—November 8, 2013

The Washington Post reported on October 29, 2013 about the inhumane treatment of poultry on the processing line. Normally, the heads of birds are electrocuted first, and then their necks are cut, followed by scalding water and de-feathering process. However, one percent of the time this goes amiss, and these birds survive until they enter the boiling water Almost a million chicken a year are alive when dunked into scalding water.

Clearly, this article appeals to the emotions of the Post's readers. Some believe this inappropriate chicken mortality to be a drastic case of "inhumane" animal killings. But in reality, chicken deaths are not foremost on our minds. After all, chicken are for eating and appear to us mostly in the form of nuggets or other compressed versions. How many of us have seen live chicken apart from those on the chicken retrieval trucks? They have to die somehow, and are, for many of us, not marked by particular attention or friendship.

Take the example of the lobster. If you go to a top of the line seafood restaurant, typically you are given the option to pick out your 'personal' lobster, live from the tank. Before it makes its way onto your plate, it will be dropped into boiling water, where, after some frantic clawing against the pot with its claws, it will die—or better—be prepared for you. Of course, lobsters can't neigh or bark, and we've always had a certain fear of being attacked by their claws—so there is not too much concern.

Think about the ocean: If tuna fishermen catch some Dolphins on the side and they die, we are most unhappy—we even require 'dolphin safe' tuna meals, if they are to come to the United States. We mourn the wounded and grieve the injuries of dolphins, because we've all seen 'Flipper", what a cute thing. At the same time we fear and resent the great white shark, which is much more endangered than dolphins. But we all remember 'jaws' and know what that fish is after.

Back to the chicken: 50 years ago, you could pick out your chicken at the market where it was beheaded in front of you. The bird would run around headless until it eventually died from blood loss. At that time, all you were worried about was dinner on your plate.

The deeper focus of this whole matter is that sometimes too much information is not seen as helpful. Ultimately, we do not want to know nor do we sufficiently care about the process of how our poultry is slaughtered. As long as the bird is sufficiently cleaned and later cooked, we will not make a fuss. It will taste the same in the end and serve the same purpose of filling our stomachs.

This same procedure and ideal can be applied to the recent NSA accusations of the United States spying on foreign nations' top officials. We simply prefer not to know and we think that foreign dignitaries should not know either, nor should they worry. Naturally, we all assumed that such spying occurred on some level, given the advances in technology in addition to national security purposes. The time when 'gentlemen did not read other gentlemen's mail' has long passed. We know what is needed and we do what needs to be done. Therefore, the question remains, were we really that surprised?

That's what chicken have in common with the NSA. As long as they give us a good product at the end, it's probably best not to discuss the process which leads to the product. After all, we're all friends.

Guilt or Competition? Winning the Cyber Espionage War

(With Alice Lu)

Originally Published in the Sri Lanka Guardian

During the Cold War, the Allies protected Germany's Fulda gap against a possible Soviet invasion. In today's environment of cyber vulnerability, surely all major parties have developed a plan of defense against cyber aggression. If not, they should do so. Yet even good plans may not fulfill the hopes of their fathers.

Remindful of Emile Zola's 'J'accuse' about anti-semitism in France, the United States has charged five officials in the Chinese People's Liberation Army of hacking into U.S. commercial computers and stealing top-secret trade information. The hackers stand accused of taking confidential nuclear and solar technology data for the benefit of their firms, thus giving Chinese businesses an unfair competitive advantage. Chinese officials have vehemently denounced these "fictitious allegations" and claim that they threaten the established mutual trust between China and the U.S.

Is this just another stalemate or what is the news here? The Chinese have collected information from the United States for quite some time, just as the Russians, Germans, and French have. It is also now common knowledge that the U.S. gathers extensive information from China as well as Germany and many other nations. Why, then, is this kerfuffle taken more seriously than routine hacking?

Some speculate that this entire affair is "running a new pig through town," a European way of referring to new actions designed to move attention away from policy failures. Perhaps we are witnessing a plan designed to distract from the current criticism of Obamacare or Veterans Affairs.

Or is this Chinese incident truly more serious than regular cyber espionage? America's displeasure seems to be based on its discovery of a linkage between security measures and industrial espionage. Security espionage benefits from an international consensus that governments have the responsibility to learn about any measures taken abroad which could endanger their own citizens. Industrial, or economic espionage however, is seen as much more unacceptable if governments intervene abroad for the sake of their businesses. The U.S. differentiates accordingly, and in light of the now great importance of international business, shares its view with other nations. The difference is also well expressed in a terminology, which clearly separates intelligence agents from spies.

If all this is a competitiveness issue, then of course proceeding against the hackers is not enough. Steps must also be taken against the users of the maliciously obtained information, since it is the use not just the possession, which causes the greatest damage.

Is America hypocritical in charging the Chinese with cyber-espionage? When the U.S. was still a young nation and the U.K. was the world leader in innovation, America also participated in espionage (and did not pay for intellectual property) in order to advance technologically. Perhaps China will ensure its protection once it has enough of its own property to protect.

Is all this only a U.S.–Chinese problem, or is industrial espionage a key problem around the world? Does the punishment reflect a special fear of Chinese reverse engineering capabilities?

There may be a new era of knowledge acquisition and distribution where military/political insights are either linked to economic/production knowledge, or are kept separate from each other. Right now, the world trend seems to be in the direction of obtaining information in all areas of human activity, and to use it for any advance possible.

The U.S. can be the key bulwark separating military and business knowledge. Sanctions against five Chinese individuals will not produce any major direct curtailment of information acquisition and use. But there can be a clear symbolic effect.

This dispute over espionage is just another demonstration of the ultimate clash between the U.S. and China. They have different perspectives of the role of the State and business. If the sanctions bring a change in the global differentiation between types and use of information, then the actions taken against the five individuals are well worth the effort. If not, we're witnessing the erasure of another line in the sand. For the sake of an internationally level playing field and the encouragement of fair competition and market driven activities, let us hope that this wake-up call stirs new thinking around the world.

The Janus Face of International Marketing

(with Charles Skuba)

Originally Published by Marketing Management—Fall 2011

Effective marketing and ethical practices must exist together.

We both are dyed-in-the-wool international marketers. Our last column explained our fervent belief in the contributions of international marketing to a better quality of life. Yet there are also fears and challenges emanating from the field and its activities. Just like the Roman god Janus, who had two faces and has come to embody the notion of contradiction to modern thinkers, international marketing brings both good and bad to the global marketplace. Exploitation of factory workers by global apparel brands exemplifies the negative consequences of globalization, but that is really more of an operations and management issue (except for the risk and impact of negative publicity on the brand). With the recent dramatic expansion of international marketing to new audiences in the developing world, there are serious social impacts that need consideration. Here are our thoughts on those, calibrated by input from global executives.

Encounter of the unexpected. Janus was not only a god of contradiction but a god whose countenance the Romans put on doors and gates as a symbol of transition. There are many who, in times of transition, have come new to market, and even new to marketing. New dimensions have made life more complex, both for marketers and those who are being marketed to. For example, some slogans offered routinely to markets with a public experienced with marketing, such as "you may have won a new car," may be interpreted quite differently by newcomers. Their high expectations may lead to disappointments and even hostility. Because marketers are the initiators of new practices, it is their responsibility to avoid causing harm.

Distorting aspirations. As economic growth in emerging markets allows millions of people to enter the middle class, it brings great new opportunities for them to improve the quality of their lives. It also exposes them to the challenge of rising aspirations with limited income. New international consumers must learn how to manage their aspirations as they experience emotional marketing appeals for products and services that might not be considered practical or "good for them."

In a chapter titled "Ethical Lapses of Marketers" in Jagdish Sheth and Rajendra Sisodia's book, *Does Marketing Need Reform?* (M.E. Sharpe, 2006), good friend Philip Kotler posed two dimensions of "the marketing dilemma" for all marketing: (1) What if the customer wants something that is not good for him or her? (2) What if the product or service, while good for the customer, is not good for society or other groups? How consumers, marketers and societies manage that dilemma in international markets will need to be resolved on a country-by-country basis.

Coping with culture. All too often, cultures are insufficiently studied or wrongly interpreted. It might seem that responsiveness to cultural differences should be second nature to marketers and therefore virtually reflexive. However, cultural differences continue to challenge marketers and can negatively affect the marketplace. Many times, disregarding local idiosyncrasies is like the introduction of a destructive virus on a culture. For example, bringing snakes to Guam almost exterminated all birds there. Or, when selling construction wood to Japan, the importer of the boards needs to consider both the typical Japanese "tsubo" size, as well as the Japanese tendency to build smaller rooms. Not doing so supports the success of competitors and leaves Japanese purchasers dissatisfied.

Though there is frequent talk about how we understand each other so much better than in the past, the reality looks different. The actual overlap between societies is typically very miniscule. There may be a number of Chinese industry leaders who have been to the United States and have developed a clear understanding of America and Americans, but they represent a very small fraction of the Chinese populace. The average Chinese person may knowledgably understand as much about Columbus, Ohio, as the average Buckeye State resident knows about Tianjin. The consequence of that limitation is a danger of misunderstandings and susceptibility to hostility.

Winner takes all. One key Western marketing dimension is the glory of victory in competition. Such an adherence to victory often means that, akin to Atilla's hordes of yesteryear, there is no mercy for the vanquished. Not everywhere are such approaches supported, desired or accepted. Often, the goal becomes for the victor to mend fences, reinvigorate a feeling of togetherness and provide a cause for standing together. In many societies it is expected that one not take advantage of what could be done, but rather consensually do what ought to be done. Such context makes it far less acceptable to practice what we have called "vampire marketing," where the airline or hotel extracts blood-sucking prices for additional services or products from its captive audience after the major purchase decision has been made. Perhaps Western marketers can learn valuable lessons from this context and consequently make themselves more valuable to their customers.

Who is on the pedestal? Particularly in the United States, we think of the individual as the key component of society. But such a perspective is not uniformly taken around the world. For example, in socialist or tribal societies it is typically the group that receives preference over the individual. Society can also be seen as the key shaper of the individual. Or perhaps the family is accorded top billing. In such cases, just imagine how different emphases in making financial decisions can be re-interpreted in various settings. What may be corruption and bribery to some may turn out to be filial devotion to others. With the strict administration of the U.S. Foreign Corrupt Practices Act and the new, more stringent U.K. anti-bribery law about to take effect, there may be harsh consequences to businesses and individuals who are not attentive to the laws governing that contradiction.

It's not personal. Distance makes the heart grow fonder, it is often said. But in international marketing, distance can also mean abdication of responsibility. Marketers sometimes clearly demonstrate their desire not to know—for example, by appointing a middleman about whose behavior one can later on be suitably astonished, surprised and mortified. As developing nations develop greater expectations of corporate social responsibility and create new legal requirements, irresponsible marketers may encounter a less tolerant face in host countries. Though the chairman of the multinational corporation may feel suitably removed from local issues, be assured that the locals take all of the firm's actions very personally.

Whose idea is it anyway? As international marketers voraciously pursue opportunity, they will also encounter fierce local competition and instant copying of good ideas. Intellectual property rights violations, including counterfeiting, piracy and copyrights violations, are rampant in many parts of the developing world. These not only harm the international marketer but also the consumers who purchase defective products. Think of the consumer who needs treatment for a critical illness and receives a fake drug. Or consider the situation of Chinese passengers after the crash of high-speed trains, which were manufactured by Chinese companies with technology incompetently copied from Western companies. The government policy of "technology importation, digestive absorption, independent re-innovation and localization" rings hollow to the grieving families of crash victims.

We can use Janus as a god of contradictions and transitions, but we can not turn to him for guidance in morality, ethics or even law. International marketers will confront dilemmas and challenges. How well they pursue the conjunction of highly effective marketing and ethical practices will inevitably be reflected in the loyalty of customers and the judgment of host governments.

Pinball—Competing Economic Aspirations

Originally Published in the Korea Times; September 11, 2008

President-elect Obama will set a new pace for the United States and for people around the world. In light of the many expectations tied to the campaign, it helps to think about competing values when it comes to their implementation.

The economic problems confronting the global economy will not disappear for the new administration. However, there will be a sense of change. Having a new team in place, with new policies yet to be formulated, is like scratching off the barnacles from the hull of a ship.

Movement will likely be faster, more flexible, and easier. There will, however, also be unexpected and unintended consequences that increase the risk of running up on the shoals.

It will be crucial to reconcile the apparent conflict between the responsible economic behavior of citizens and the responsible leadership of the economy. The message of `save more', for example, was always helpful for economic stability.

Yet, for the sake of economic growth, the necessarily complementary message of `spend less' was unacceptable in the past. With new excitement about social obligation, now may be the right time to offer and implement opportunities for sacrifice.

There is need for a national agreement that excessive expenditure, wars, and high commodity prices must result in dialing back expectations, expenditures, and excess. Active consumer expenditures will be important to keep the economy going.

The recent steep decline in vehicle sales demonstrates the disadvantages of too much consumer caution. One needs to prevent individuals and society from becoming cheap. Greater selectivity based on quality should be a key focus of enlightened self-interest.

There will be less reliance on market forces. But if one does not use market signals, there needs to be the development of secondary indicators.

Accepting new and different non-market criteria will encourage the productivity of think tanks, government offices and universities and provide for greater flexibility. At the same time, there will be an increase in policy errors, performance uncertainty and outcome disputes.

Less faith in free markets will affect currency values and exchange rates. Government will intervene more quickly and perhaps more severely to reach desired currency values. Such extraterritorial application of policy goals will be a new drawback for foreign trading partners.

The business orientation of politics will not have the same high priority as in the recent past. A reduced linkage between policy and trade will provide allies with less preferential treatment and less market access.

Domestic change will affect international perspectives. Consider traditional core dimensions of American capitalism, such as risk, competition, profit and property. For example, the risk/reward relationship is likely to become less central to decision-making, resulting in new goals and narrower ranges of outcomes.

A reduction in incentives for competition may lead to more harmony, but perhaps also reduce the speed of innovation. More creative thinking about property rights will provide for more flexibility in the development of medications, but may precipitate the global migration of pharmaceutical firms.

Think of it in terms of a traditional pinball machine: Currently, when a player achieves a high score in competition, the machine issues an extra ball—which allows the winner to further extend his lead.

Now consider what would happen if the player who falls behind, receives the extra ball in order to catch up with the leader. Such a shift would not necessarily be uninteresting, but would produce very different rules of the game.

Then there is the key issue of paying for all the desired changes. Past decades of government policy have focused on reducing inflation. The new focus on employment generation will require a neglect of inflation concerns in favor of stimulative expenditures.

Over time, the budget implications of such a shift will require to substantially broaden public income. Doing so will be difficult, given the key commitments already made in the area of tax policy.

In addition, such measures are likely to further affect the value of the U.S. brand, leading to more reticence of foreign direct investment.

There are also new expectations for higher standards of virtue, vision and veracity by individuals, corporations and government in order to restore faith and confidence. Yet, both domestically and internationally such values cannot be created overnight, but rather require gradual shifts in perspectives and cultures.

Regardless of the desire for quick action, an era of globalization demands the harmonization of approaches in order to eliminate the jockeying for local advantage.

The times are new, but the inspiration for how to shoulder leadership is not. Two millennia ago St. Paul, also called the 13th Apostle, provided a good example. Saul, as he was also known, was a Jew who converted to Christianity. He was born in Tarsus, and therefore a Roman citizen.

He was an indefatigable traveler, an early globalist who wrote many letters. During his life and travels, he often confronted objections, even hostility and persecution. Whenever the odiousness became too intense—his claim to Roman citizenship gave his message power and saved his life more than once.

The new administration faces competing goals domestically and internationally. Many people in this world want to like America. Global leadership has too often been sidetracked by narrow concerns.

Inner strength, skills, and morality are essential for long-term leadership for the common good. Paul's message appears to have had staying power. May the years to come provide us all with social progress and reward.

SECTION 6

On Exports

Exports and Innovation

Originally Published by Marketing Management—Spring 2011

Recently I participated in a conference sponsored by the National Academies of the United States, and the German Institute for Economic Research (DIW). Participants were international luminaries such as John Holdren, Science Advisor to President Obama, Klaus Scharioth, German Ambassador to the United States, Andreas Pinkwart, former Minister for Innovation, Science, Research and Technology of Nordrhein Westphalia and Klaus Zimmermann, President of the DIW.

The meeting focused on an analysis and comparison of US-German innovation policies. Research transforms money into knowledge, while innovation converts knowledge into money. Substantial discussions of the two day event centered on manufacturing and trade and the lessons for export policy.

The Germans highlighted their consistent surplus since World War II, fundamentally based on restrained consumption, high savings, and ongoing innovation. Current U.S. demands for a decrease in this export orientation were seen as a scary Halloween exercise at best. Market responsiveness and continued innovation was seen to support an ongoing strong German export emphasis.

Ron Bloom, presidential counselor for Manufacturing policy and automotive industry czar at the Treasury Department, stressed the importance of heading in the right direction—even when the specifics can only be worked out as they surface. He uses a small "p" in his planning and emphasizes the need for a strong manufacturing sector, with innovation playing to a country's strength. Government's role is to bridge market gaps—and to support the eventual re-emergence of market forces.

The meeting achieved some consensus, but there were also different perspectives which may lead to alternative futures for global exports:

After 50 years, the United States can no longer remain the largest market for global exports. New growth opportunities must arise elsewhere. With exchange rates driving trade, new currency theories and values will be a key policy issue. The Plaza Agreement of the 1980's was only a start for a long adjustment of the U.S. dollar.

The U.S. policy directive is clear: President Obama wants U.S. exports to double within the next five years. But many uncertainties exist. Should trade be a public concern, or be placed in the hands of trusted specialists? Is there a wheel of internationalization, with gradual declines and rises? Who is part of the ride and how does innovation drive the wheel? Is manufacturing a diminishing component in post-industrial societies? Even flexible economies experience large displacement effects of trade on individuals and regions. How does one provide appropriate and financially prudent adjustment assistance? Exports are typically supported by either decreasing risk (e.g. through information services) or increasing rewards (e.g. through tax deferrals). How to ensure that such support will actually increase exports? Should government programs support innovations directly, or are indirect effects such as an increase in management capabilities more efficient? How to educate the public on international trade issues and the need for innovation? Should established TV programs develop episodes about the receipt of a first international order? How about a national competition for firms and managers who have overcome obstacles in international markets from which we all can learn?

Global leadership requires a strong economy supported by innovation, entrepreneurship and expansion. Forced import cutbacks can reduce trade deficits, but at a substantial cost to society. Export expansion offers more payoffs, but requires continuous excellence in innovation.

Today, U.S. exports are roughly 8 percent of global trade. To balance the U.S. current account, this world market share needs to rise to 12 percent under condition of stable imports. To achieve such an increase one needs focus on what differentiates the players, and how the differences can be strengthened through innovation. Without such efforts, global competitors appear unwilling to reduce their participation in trade. Success through strength and collaboration based on a systems perspective will raise efficiencies, lessen friction and increase the global standard of living. We have to understand variations in trade needs by country, industry, and culture. We need to accept and accommodate differences in expectations. The goal must be to make firms and managers stronger, on the corporate level through innovation, and on the individual level through rising commitment and capabilities.

The Rationale for Export Promotion

Originally Published by Marketing Management—Winter 2012

Exports are important. Yet, why should firms be enticed into exporting through the use of public funds? Profit opportunities for exporters should be enough of an incentive for firms to export.

First off, it is helpful to understand the export process within the firm. Typically, firms evolve along different stages to become experienced exporters. They start out being uninterested in things international. Management frequently will not even fill an unsolicited export order. Should international market stimuli continue over time, however, a firm may move to the stage of export awareness, or even export interest. Management will begin to accumulate information about international markets and may consider the feasibility of exporting. At the export trial stage, the firm will fill selected export orders, serve a few customers, and expand into countries that are geographically close or culturally similar to the home country. At the export evaluation stage, firms consider the impact of exporting on overall corporate activities. Unless initial expectations are met, the firm is likely to discontinue its export efforts, seek alternative international growth opportunities or restrict itself to the domestic market. Success will lead the firm over time, to become an export adapter, make frequent shipments to many customers in more countries, and incorporate international considerations into its planning.

Here are my conclusions about the seven dimensions that should guide export assistance efforts, in particular where new and growing businesses are concerned. One needs to determine what export assistance is to achieve. Some of the current objectives are global fairness and the opening of world markets. Public funds and government attention are too scarce to invest solely to right wrongs or for the sake of fairness. The key focus must be on the benefits to U.S. employment.

The time frame involved should be a long-term orientation, which concentrates efforts on introducing more and new firms to the global market. Export assistance needs to achieve either a specific reduction of risk or an increase in profits for firms. It should be concentrated primarily in those areas where profit and risk inconsistencies produce market gaps, and be linked directly to identifiable organizational or managerial characteristics that need improvement. Otherwise, assistance supports only exports that would have taken place anyway. The measurement of success should be based on the export involvement of the firm, focusing on the number of customers, transactions, and locations served.

Coordination is crucial. Within government, one must avoid that well established industry sectors with relatively low employment effects consume resources in an over proportionate fashion while priority growth industries would be left to seek export success on their own with insufficient support. Externally, export assistance must ensure that the policy gains abroad are actually used by domestic firms.

Rather than concentrate only on well entrenched industries, the focus must be on sunrise industries. Export assistance should emphasize those areas where government can bring a particular strength to bear-such as contacts or prowess in opening doors abroad, or information collection capabilities. Externally, programs should aim at the large opportunities abroad. As far as firms are concerned, attention should not assist industries in trouble, but mainly help successful firms do better.

Export assistance programs should start out by analyzing the current level of international involvement of the firm and then deliver assistance appropriate to the firm's needs. For example, help with after-sales service delivery is most appropriate for firms at the adaptation stage; firms at the awareness stage worry much more about information and mechanics. Assistance must also take foreign market conditions and foreign buyer preferences into account. It is easier to sell what is in demand rather than being guided by what's in ample supply. There should be a spark of boldness which goes beyond ensuring that things are done right, but checks whether one can do more right things. One could, for example, think about domestic and international efforts to set standards for technology and quality, and include the grading of enzymes, meats, hormones, and other products developed by biotechnology firms. Or one could think about the development of a national forfeiting institution and the delivery of training to banks, to be of major assistance in handling the financial and documentation aspects of exporting.

In a world of shifting goal posts and rapidly changing realities, all firms should be prepared for the global marketplace. If they can grow and successfully meet international competition, they will strengthen themselves and the nation.

How Should We Measure the Winners?

Originally Published by Ovi
Magazine—August 8, 2012

The recent Olympics presented some interesting perspectives on competition: How do we find out who is actually winning? Is performance to be measured by wealth (medals), by leadership (Gold only) or by industry competitiveness (e.g. gymnastics)? Should the progress over time play a major role, or the number of winners as a proportion of population?

In business terms, the expression 'competitiveness' is viewed differently by different parties. For example, for a firm, competitiveness means expansion, growth and profits. Whether any of these originate in or outside of a 'home' country plays a secondary role. When governments assess the competitiveness issue, the search is for employment growth, wide income distribution and tax revenue, and location is important for all of them. Individuals, in turn, think mainly about whether or not they will keep their jobs and have their standard of living increase. For them, location is not just one thing, it is the only thing.

Sport contests reflect capability, enjoyment and the creation of goodwill, but there are other facets as well. Performance on the sports field can affect and even transform the national spirit. It is hard to forget the national triumphant feeling in the United States in 1980 when the U.S. ice hockey team beat the Soviet Union in the same year the Soviets invaded Afghanistan.

International sports performance can also be a political gesture and a test of national virtue. For example, four decades ago when President Richard Nixon and the U.S. ping pong team visited China, the US-Sino relationship was officially established. At that time, China was considered an emerging economy and a Chinese excellence in a rather narrow sport was not seen as significant. Now, although the U.S. is still the largest economy in the world, China is catching up and China's teams receive global attention. Its economy is the second largest in the world and its market is the U.S.'s third largest export destination, after Canada and Mexico.

The composition of trade between the two countries, just like the composition of the winning teams at the Olympics, has changed and demonstrated that the two economies have become more integrated than expected. In fact, China is the only nation which imports U.S. products at the level President Obama envisioned in 2009 when he postulated that U.S. exports should double in five years. U.S. top exports to China are some agricultural crops, but also electronic and mechanical appliances, chemicals, and transportation equipment such as automobiles and airplanes. China is now General Motors' most important market.

When China imports those manufactured goods, it assembles them and then ships them to other markets around the world, including to the U.S. market. If China's exports drop, the demand for U.S. goods will also drop, leading to a slower growth of U.S. exports (just like the participation of fewer athletes in the Olympics makes for less interesting games).

Rule changes also have a great effect on competition. In the Olympics, the definition of what constitutes an 'amateur' has changed over time and has led to an increase in the number of full time athletes and to an improvement in individual performance. Similarly, what counts as a performance enhancing drug matters a lot and can lead to the disqualification of athletes. The business equivalent here is the value of the Chinese currency. Even though the Renminbi has depreciated in the last few months, many see the currency value as a determinant of Chinese competitiveness and therefore a primary issue that needs to be changed. Similarly, export control systems in both countries take on a growing role and sometimes even appear to play out in a "tit-for-tat" game. For example, when the U.S. curbs high-tech product exports to China, China limits its rare earth exports in return. Just when the two economies are becoming deeply integrated, the US–China relationship is fraying, says former secretary of the treasury Henry Paulson, Jr.

It seems that policy decisions were more easily made when China was still a third-world country and the U.S.'s leading position was not challenged. With China moving up the scale economically and politically, there is the temptation to view China as a potential threat and adversary. However, just like the Olympic rivalry for medals, the issue to argue over should not be who has the largest overall GDP, or who exports more to whom. The world economy is becoming increasingly integrated, and we should not look for development and leadership in all fields, but rather in fields of specific capabilities and advantages. Just as with the Olympic Games, it doesn't matter who wins the largest number of medals; what matters is that preparation and training, competitive encounters, and excellence can lead to a more inspired and better world.

Have Lunch or Be Lunch: Smaller Firms Thrive in Vulnerable Markets

(With Ilkka Ronkainen)

Marketing Management
March—April 2003

THE UNITED STATES IS IN a vulnerable position when it comes to international trade. Since 1975, it has been importing more goods than it has been exporting, therefore running a continuous merchandise trade deficit. Even though overall U.S. exports surpassed $1 trillion in 2001, the deficit in the trade of goods was more than $426 billion. Ongoing annual trade deficits of this magnitude are unsustainable in the long run.

Such deficits add to the U.S. international debt, which must be serviced through interest payments and eventually perhaps even repaid. Therefore, an export performance by U.S. firms that matches or even exceeds our imports will become crucial.

Furthermore, exports are also an important contributor to national employment. We estimate that $1 billion of exports supports the creation, on average, of about 11,500 jobs. In its latest benchmark study, the U.S. Department of Commerce reports there were more than 8 million U.S. jobs sustained by the export of manufactured goods, which ties one out of every five U.S. manufacturing jobs directly or indirectly to exports. For example, in the state of Illinois alone, more than 360,000 jobs were linked to manufactured exports. An increase in exports can therefore be a key factor in maintaining domestic job growth.

Many see the global market as the exclusive realm of large, multinational corporations. Overlooked are the hundreds of thousands of smaller firms that have been fueling a U.S. export boom, which has supported the economy in times of limited domestic growth. The latest information from the trade data project at the Department of Commerce indicates that, between 1987 and 1999, the number of U.S. firms that export at least occasionally has more than tripled to more than 231,000. Almost 97% of these exporters were small or mid-sized companies.

The reason for the export success of smaller firms lies in the new determinants of competitiveness, as framed by the wishes and needs of the foreign buyers. Other than price, buyers today also expect an excellent product fit, high levels of corporate responsiveness, a substantial service orientation, and high corporate commitment. Small and mid-sized firms stack up well on all these dimensions, compared to their larger brethren, and may even have a competitive advantage.

Corporate Vulnerabilities

In spite of many advantages, smaller firms face major obstacles to international market prosperity.

Financial issues. All firms worry about getting paid when they ship their merchandise abroad, but small and mid-sized exporters are particularly at risk. They need financing to cover the time lag between shipping and payment receipts as well as to offer credit to buyers. Longer distances, slower transportation, and more accommodating payment terms abroad make international transactions more expensive. These transactions also require more capital and represent a larger portion of the firm's resources than do domestic transactions. In addition, due to their size, international shipments often represent a larger degree of risk than smaller firms are willing or able to tolerate.

Exchange rate changes present a major source of vulnerability. Time passes between the initiation of an international transaction and its consummation. During that time, the firm is exposed to the effects of currency shifts. Major changes of currency value can transform a good business transaction into a money-losing one.

One particular issue U.S. exporters must cope with is the competition from the Euro zone and its currency volatility. The Euro is the new international trade currency the European Union implemented widely on in 2002. Even though originally introduced at a value slightly higher than the dollar, the Euro was valued at only .88 during most of 2002. Consequently, U.S. imports from Europe became cheaper, but U.S. exporters found it more difficult to compete. During the latter part of last year, the Euro rose in value and now exceeds the dollar. However, this has mainly been a function of different interest rate policies, which have been guided by a flexible U.S. Fed and a very unyielding European Central Bank. Changes in bank leadership, which appear quite likely, may presage new policies and a return to a rapidly rising dollar.

Smaller firms also lack the unfettered access to global capital markets that large firms have. They still rely very heavily on mainly domestic or even local sources of money. As a result, they don't benefit from the low-cost opportunities of global capital and are not diversified enough in their sources of funds to cope with local interest rate inefficiencies. Given the increasing commoditization of goods, price shifts resulting from interest or exchange rate changes may critically affect the firm's competitiveness and profits.

Supply chain management. Key concerns here are the development of contacts, relationships, and networks with suppliers and the forging of a systems linkage with intermediaries and customers. In addition, there are the logistics of arranging transportation, determining transport rates, handling documentation, obtaining financial information, coordinating distribution, packaging, and obtaining insurance. The logistics are often handled by intermediaries, such as freight forwarders. This area also includes the overseas servicing of exports, where the firm needs to accommodate returns and provide parts, repair service, and technical advice. Often the solution is to open a servicing or distribution office abroad. Timely communication among the different members of the supply chain is crucial if a firm is to perform competitively. Here again, small and mid-sized firms are particularly vulnerable since they may need to invest heavily in information technology—a major capital outlay. They don't have the clout of large firms that can require their international supply chain members to adapt to a standardized information system. Smaller firms have to adapt to multiple systems and find ways to make them internationally compatible—incurring additional expenses and technical difficulties.

Firms that developed elaborate just-in-time delivery systems for their international shipments were also severely affected by the border and port closures during the days following the terrorist attacks on the United States. Together with their service providers, they continue to be affected by the increased security measures. Firms now need to focus on internal security and must demonstrate to third parties how much more security-oriented they've become. In many instances, government authorities require evidence of threat-reduction efforts to speed things along. Insurance companies have increased their premiums substantially in response to new definitions of risk. Unless policy holders take major steps to reduce such risk (or assume some of it themselves), they are likely to suffer from continued premium increases.

Regulatory issues. Another key vulnerability consists of legal procedures and typically covers government red tape, product liability, licensing, and customs/duty issues. Here, small and mid-sized firms are particularly exposed to changing government policies. The September 11 terrorist attacks have profoundly affected the administration of U.S. export controls and customs procedures. While larger firms have the benefit of a fully staffed department that deals with regulatory affairs, smaller exporters often face new and unfamiliar territory. For them, export control regulations are more burdensome. In addition, customs classifications and rules may require the hiring of specialists who ensure that shipments go out and come in properly reported and on time.

On the regulatory side, U.S. firms also are exposed to the vicissitudes of trade policy. Market access and market performance issues should be taken up in the Doha Round, the new conference of trade liberalization negotiations due to conclude by 2005. However, in existing trade disputes, our firms are also threatened by the retaliatory measures taken by trade adversaries overseas. Even though a conflict may be totally unrelated to their industry, U.S. manufacturers are vulnerable to foreign trade policy actions specifically designed to elicit the largest amount of pain from their victims. For example, when European countries or China react to U.S. import duties on foreign steel products, they do so by placing new (or higher) tariffs on a wide range of U.S. products. This makes many U.S. firms, including smaller producers, noncompetitive in these markets. They, in effect, pay the price for the U.S. protection of the domestic steel industry.

Market contact. Small to mid-sized firms need to cope with advertising, sales effort, and obtaining marketing information. They also need to develop foreign market intelligence on the location of markets, trade restrictions, and competitive conditions overseas. For large firms, such activities are often part of market expansion, where additional activities are carried out in already familiar territory. Small and mid-sized firms, however, are often still at the level of international market entry, where each step requires the dedication of new resources to unfamiliar tasks. It bears remembering that any new entrant into the international market must not only match, but must exceed by far, the capabilities of the local competition overseas. After all, apart from needing to find the spare capacity among its management resources, which permits a corporate focus on and commitment to exports, the newcomer must also carry all the transaction costs associated with the internationalization process. These start with the cost of shipping and special packaging and include duties and other special international burdens.

All these obstacles, both real and perceived, can prevent firms from exporting. Many managers often see only the risks involved rather than the opportunities the international market can present. As a result, the United States still under-exports when compared to other nations. U.S. merchandise exports comprise only 11% of GDP, compared to 28.3% for Germany and 25.4% for the United Kingdom. On a per capita basis, in 2000 the United Kingdom exported $6,226 for every man, woman, and child. The figure for Germany was $7,498, and for the United States, only $3,878.

Opportunities for Support

Currently, U.S. export performance is insufficient given its potential. Many small and medium-sized exporters are too complacent to globalize because they're either content with a vast domestic market or fear the complexity of selling abroad. Firms that do consider global opportunities appear to be unwilling to initiate major expansions of their operations abroad because of their real and perceived risk in the international market.

One core business concern is financing. On the positive side, private lenders of trade finance are becoming more active in the United States, but they often lend at relatively high rates. U.S. exporters have the benefit of many effective federal and state government programs, such as the working capital guarantee program by the Export Import Bank of the United States (Eximbank), which provides financing assistance. There are several programs specifically designed to help small business exporters. Still there needs to be a continuous emphasis on small business lending support and a responsible adaptation of credit criteria for the conditions of small and medium-sized enterprises. For example, small and mid-sized firms often can't afford to provide all the detailed evaluations and documentations lenders ideally want to see.

Of key relevance is a stable financial environment, both domestically and internationally. Small and mid-sized firms can cope with changing conditions. However, the speed of change can severely influence or even destroy the profitability of operations. Any policy measures that affect the access to and the cost of capital of smaller firms or the exchange rate of the dollar should specifically take into account the consequences and burden that such steps would impose on U.S. exporters.

Think Internationally

In time, nearly every firm will be an international marketer, by default if not by design. As globalization expands, companies will have no place to hide. New foreign competition in their own backyards will force firms to think internationally, if only defensively. Improving offerings to combat new rivals at home might well generate new demand for a firm's goods in foreign markets. As online marketplaces bring together buyers and sellers from all over the world quickly and efficiently, Internet search engines will lead prospective customers to company Web sites, even those designed for domestic buyers only.

From most perspectives, world trade conducted by savvy international marketers is the prerequisite to global growth, prosperity, and freedom for all peoples. And for companies themselves, the choice is clear: Have lunch or be lunch.

Eagles Fly But Don't Always Soar

Originally Published by Liechtensteiner Vaterland— February 11, 2008

The world's stock markets experience a decline. Sharp drops of shares occurred in Hong Kong, Istanbul and Frankfurt, and many seem to blame the United States and the market approach as the causes for their predicament.

Commentators now predict a serious global recession for all markets. The U.S. is singled out with additional forecasts promising a steep drop of the U.S. dollar, sharp reductions in U.S. military strength and vanishing of U.S. political influence. Alas, these commentators are sadly mistaken.

All too often, forecasters are looking only at the short term. Their long term usually means next week. Yet, the world turns much slower than the typical media blurb makes us believe.

Countries adjust their strategies only gradually, as do most customers, entrepreneurs, and corporations. Rather than being driven by momentary shifts, sensible thinkers search for a context, and look at the road rather than the turnoff.

Take the current changes in share values. Financial markets have changed for many years—and typically, in the past few decades, it has been for the better. Families, towns, provinces and nations have improved their lot.

Health care has improved, both in terms of pharmaceuticals and in care delivery. Housing has become better, and education, a crucial ingredient of progress and growth, now reaches many more than ever before. Incomes are strong .

Today, there is much more ability to achieve, accomplish, and to accumulate. There is less famine, more opportunity and more freedom. Life is best it's been in millennia.

It is human nature to strive upward and therefore not be satisfied with the status quo. But such a drive should concentrate not just on a few select economic issues of the moment.

We have even come to the point where mere stability and constancy is seen as wrong and as indicative of "falling behind."

Imagine an executive who told his shareholders that he wants his company's sales to remain stable—most analysts would probably run him over on their way to other firms. But isn't stability in itself worthwhile and good? What ever happened to catching one's breadth!

As children, many of us read stories and books about "getting ready for a rainy day." By doing so, there was no implication that temporary setbacks were a fatal disease. Rather, there was an acceptance, forged from experience with Mother Nature that there are seasons, and that life has its ups and downs.

Even eagles occasionally descend to lower heights so that they can catch an updraft and soar again. There is nothing to be ashamed of if resources have to be rearranged and if one accepts that not everything is linear.

Think of growth in the context of angles on a protractor: Growth does not always have to take place at all degrees, on all levels, and simultaneously.

For those who see the U.S. and the benefits of the market approach which it has propagated, in steep decline, let them look at history, as sensible people do.

For example, in a recent discussion of global economics, a Chinese acquaintance readily agreed that his nation had perhaps had a bad run which lasted a century, but he assured me that China was now ready to again become the center of the world.

Think of the long term and ongoing contributions of the United States to world economic growth and welfare. In the 1940s, the country pioneered the three key international organizations which form the pillars of world trade and investment: The International Monetary Fund (IMF), the World Bank, and the World Trade Organization (WTO).

Without them, the world economy could never have reached its current level of success. Through joint efforts on the exchange rate front and a willingness to rely on market based exchange rates, the U.S. ensured growing money supply which has led to rising economic abundance.

The country's willingness to be the largest marketplace to the world has provided opportunities for innovation, growth, profit, and enjoyment to many. And all this has been achieved within a system which provides for political adjustments and transitions without unchecked power, bloody battles or economic destruction.

The U.S. remains the land of opportunity where one can realize dreams under open skies. It continues to be a key destination for immigrants, because they know that vision is admired, that effort is rewarded, and that achievement is supported.

There is security and safety in the land, and there is flexibility to adjust to new conditions. Even in times of temporary setbacks, the outlook is bright.

Trust, promise and the future that a nation offers to those holding its investments, its currency and its contracts are the long-term key dimensions which define global leadership. Those who believe that the U.S. is in terminal decline should remember that the Roman Empire lasted more than 700 years, the Ottoman Empire almost 600, Britain's for 350 years.

They too had their ebb and flow, and they demonstrated that good expectations for the longer-term future together with internal cohesion provided sufficient impetus for continuing success. The best is yet to come!

Index

www.ingramcontent.com/pod-product-compliance
Lightning Source LLC
Chambersburg PA
CBHW031328210326
41519CB00048B/3624